DO YOU KNOW THE TRUTH?

JAMES MIAN

ISBN 978-1-956001-61-7 (paperback)
ISBN 978-1-956001-62-4 (eBook)

Copyright © 2021 by James Mian

All rights reserved. No part of this publication may be reproduced, distributed, or transmitted in any form or by any means, including photocopying, recording, or other electronic or mechanical methods without the prior written permission of the publisher.

Printed in the United States of America

CONTENTS

Introduction		v
1.	The Gift	1
2.	Set Free	4
3.	Jesus Wants to Save Our Souls	8
4.	Press On. Hang in there!	12
5.	The Answer: It Starts With Me	15
6.	The Answer to Sin: The Answer Lies in Saying No	19
7.	Anger: What God Says About Anger	23
8.	Believers, Doubters, Mockers	28
9.	Being Critical	33
10.	Bible Studies	36
11.	Challenges	40
	a. Circle of Healing	43
	b. Commitment	46
	c. Am I Committed?	48
12.	Condemnation	53
	a. Running	57
13.	Conviction	61
	a. Day Of The Lord	63
14.	Deeper Hurts: Learning to Let Go	68
	a. Depression	72
	b. Devil	76
	c. Discipline	79
15.	Encouragement	83
	a. Look For The Good In People	86

16. Disagreements 89
    a. Philemon 94
17. Expectations 97
    a. Eternal Life 100
    b. Surviving Judgment 104
18. Election and Justification 108
    a. Redemption, Sanctification, and Glorification 111
    b. Law and Grace 115
19. Who Does God Want Us To Be? 119
    a. Walking in the Light 122
    b. What the World Needs 126
    c. How Does God Measure Greatness 128
20. Fear of God 131
    a. Feeling Defeated 135
    b. Fellowship 139
    c. Finances 142
    d. Finances 2 144
    e. Forgiveness 147
    f. Hope: Hard Times 151
    g. Humility 154
21. Illness 158
22. Limitations 161
    a. Learning To Resist Temptation 163
    b. Loneliness 167
    c. Psalm 32 172
    d. Prayer 174
23. Who's Right, Who's Wrong? 180
24. Time To Change 183
25. To the Oppressed 188
26. Feed My Sheep 192
27. A Living Sacrifice (ESV) 196
28. Keep Your Eyes On Me 200
29. Thank You, Jesus 203
30. God's Answer To the World 207
About the Author 213

INTRODUCTION

Why did I write, "Do You Know the Truth?" I wrote, hoping you can see the way God answers our prayers. He doesn't always answer our prayers by giving us what we want; He answers them by giving us what we need. Through time's like we are facing, I have learned to ask God for what I need.

I wrote, "Do You Know the Truth," hoping people realize God is a forgiving God. He accepts you, and He loves you. He doesn't want to change you, but He gives you choices on how you want to live your life. God wants you to become stronger in areas you are weak. No matter how far you have fallen, God is waiting with open arms to help you.

Even if you feel your life is hopeless, God can do the impossible. My God doesn't break His promises. God is greater than anything we are facing in the world today. "For I am convinced that neither death nor life, neither angels and demons, neither the present nor the future, nor any powers, neither height nor depth, nor anything else in all creation, will be able to separate us from the love of God that is in Christ Jesus our Lord,(Romans 8:38-39.)"

I wrote much of this book while America and the world are going through the coronavirus. I can't believe the sadness and the heartache we are going through. People are dying; our lives are being affected in many ways. Despite everything, God is still giving me hope of a better tomorrow.

I realize life can all be taken away from us in a moment. The coronavirus is a wake-up call for many in the world today. At times like this, I began to realize what is essential in my life. Right now, I value gratitude and how Jesus gives me hope in trying times. God is answering my prayers by giving me what I need. If it all gets taken away, I still have God and my salvation. God is greater than he (Satan) that rules most of the world today. God is greater than the coronavirus that is affecting people around the globe.

I hope people take the time to pray and find a God who can give them the strength and will to keep moving forward. I pray people don't look at what they are losing but what they can gain. God is building a stronger faith in those who believe in Him. You might not see the good today, but some good will come out of all this.

I can think about what I am losing or thank God for the hope He is giving me. Right now, bad things are happening to good people. I am praying for God to give everyone hope. If they are losing their business, I pray God will help them keep moving forward, and when the time comes, help them rebuild all that they have lost. I want people to know, regardless of how you feel about God, that he loves you and wants to help you.

Many of the people coming into our churches need help. What they need are love and compassion. They need to be heard and accepted. They come with failed marriages; some have lost the love of their family and friends. Even gays are coming into our church; they don't need signs telling them they aren't welcome. Everyone who comes into our churches seeking God should be honored. We never know how the Holy Spirit will change their lives. We don't write their story; we are merely a messenger of God's word, and God wants us to feed His sheep.

Jesus Christ is the answer to the brokenness in the world today. God looked into the future, and He knew we would need redemption. People are coming back and are being filled with the Holy Spirit. The Holy Spirit is changing lives and helping them to move forward.

DO YOU KNOW THE TRUTH?

While reading this book, I pray you to put all your prejudice aside and learn about a loving God. I implore any walls you have toward God to fall. God is rebuilding His church based on Jesus and His principles. This book is not about religion; this is about Jesus and how He lived His life. Regardless of how far you have fallen or any situation that has come into your life, Jesus wants you to know the truth; His truth will set you free!

CHAPTER 1

The Gift

The gift isn't always getting what you want. The award is getting what we need. Many people base their happiness on getting the things they want. We want what we want, and we want it now!

When my wife and I were coming back from up north, I had a warning. My wife hasn't heard anything from her daughter. The alarm was that something had happened to my stepdaughter. Two days later, my wife found her daughter on her apartment floor. She had passed away. Trinity was 23 years old. She had overdosed on a medication the therapist gave her for depression. Three years before I met her, her youngest son Erick died in a car accident. My wife is a strong spiritual woman; she wouldn't have survived without her faith in God.

I was grateful I could be a support for my wife. We gave Trinity a funeral her friends and relatives would remember. For once in our marriage, I honestly did the right things. I don't regret the money I spent coming from a man who hated spending money; that was a small miracle. When I had that warning, the little voice inside me told me I would have to spend some money. I think God has spoken to me twice in my life; this was the first time.

Romans 8:28: "And we know in all things God works for the good of those who love Him, who have been called according to His purpose."

Losing Trinity was one of the things that happened in my life that would lead me to Jesus. However, until I made Jesus my Lord and Savior, I didn't know the meaning of the verse above. How could God make any good come out of the deaths that have happened to my wife?

Nothing can be more painful for a mother than to bury her children at such a young age. Our marriage hit bottom; deep down, I didn't realize how much she was suffering. I knew I was losing her. I didn't know how I could pull us back together.

My wife and I like to dance, so we joined a dance class in Utica, Michigan. The teachers' Herb and Kathy, welcomed us with so much love and kindness. The whole group was friendly, and we developed some relationships with the couples in the group. After a short time, we would attend one of their church services. Looking back, this was God's way of introducing us to Christianity.

God knows us better than we know ourselves. He knew we were ready to become a part of His purpose. I saw a lot of the people at Church who were part of our dance group. Since meeting Herb and Kathy, I know of five couples who became members of the Church. That doesn't include many people who attend the events the Church puts on annually. Visiting the Church on Sunday, I felt I found a place to call home. Eventually, this would lead to making Jesus my Lord and Savior. From the moment I met Jesus, our life as husband and wife began to change.

It took time for God to help us. Just because we were Christians didn't mean we wouldn't have problems. God helped me by showing me my role in this marriage. He taught me certain boundaries, and I learned how to let go. There were things about my wife; I couldn't change or fix. God showed me the battles; I needed to fight.

Eventually, my friend and I started a Bible study group in our neighborhood. I watched my Christian friends go through some painful situations. Being there for each other was a blessing we all could share. Since becoming a Christian, I have met people genuinely suffering, but there was peace around them that only God could place in their spirit. I learned the energy inside them is the Holy Spirit. Because of their faith in God, their lives could keep moving forward. Through my struggles, I realized that he could put His light into any darkness that has come into my life. The pain would draw me closer to God, and my faith in Him would get stronger.

People use God's name in vain. People blame God for all the pain and suffering in the world. People make fun of God and say the people who believe in Him are weak. When they see people praying, they say: "What good is prayer." People don't understand God and His purpose. That was why I wanted to write, "Do you know the Truth."

We all have troubles. God is teaching me in ways that lead to peace and understanding. He is changing me into the person I was created to be. The gift God has given me doesn't mean He will answer all my wants. The award is the hope, the strength, and the ability to change: These are the things I need. The forgiveness and joy Jesus has put inside me keep my life moving forward. Jesus is teaching me a way to live. I have principles that I can follow. My life has purpose and meaning. God is taking the brokenness and changing it into victory. I have a personal relationship with God, and Jesus has given me a way to live my life.

I pray that everyone who reads this book will feel the joy that God can put into their lives. God wants His glory to shine in everyone's life. God can take your brokenness and help you to move forward!

I am 69 years old. I am learning to be a better husband and dealing with a son who doesn't want my help. Finding Jesus has helped me see what I need, and the Holy Spirit inside me shows me what I can do. I can't fix everyone, so God has given me the strength to let go. I have been sober and off of any street drugs for over thirty-five years, but it took me all those years before I met Jesus. We can be drug-free but still in a fog. Getting sober is only a percent of the problem; the other 99% is learning how to live. Jesus showed me a way to live, a move that would lead me to eternal freedom!

CHAPTER 2

Set Free

Lamentations 1:14: "My sins have been bound into a yoke; by His hands they were woven together. They have come upon my neck, and the LORD has sapped my strength, He has handed me over to those I cannot withstand."

Lamentation is a book written by Jeremiah; he was one of God's prophets. He was telling the Israelites that when they disobey God, they will invite trouble into their lives. Sin at first gives us the illusion we are free, but that kind of freedom can lead us away from God.

The ultimate price for sin is punishment. Jeremiah was mourning for Jerusalem; their sins were pulling them away from God and the freedom only God could give them. The Israelites became captive to sin and bound by sin's yoke. Without God's help, their enemies could overtake them.

Lamentations 2:11: "My eyes fail from weeping, I am in torment within, my heart is poured out on the ground because my people are destroyed, because children and infants faint in the streets of the city." You can feel the sorrow Jeremiah was feeling. How many of us are in torment, knowing the world is falling apart?

If you look around our world, it is indeed falling apart. The morals and principles of society are changing. People are creating a God of their own making. The truth that has governed our nation is being torn apart by the government. We are substituting the truth (fact) for a lie. Looking back into history, I find myself no better than the Israelites when it comes to God and how He wanted us to live. Looking at the world, in general, it feels like it is falling apart.

Before meeting Jesus, my sins had me bound in a yoke. There is nothing more painful than watching your life fall apart, and it seems nothing you do can change it. I didn't know how to stop this from happening. I was sick and tired of losing and having to start over once again. Going to God and learning about Jesus was the beginning that would set me free. Finding Jesus gave me hope; God's forgiveness gave me comfort. Yes, I was humble enough to admit I needed help!

Galatians 5:13-15: "You, my brothers, were called to be free. But do not use your freedom to indulge the sinful nature; rather, serve one another in love. The entire law is summed up in a single command: 'Love your neighbor as yourself.' If you keep on biting and devouring each other, watch out or you will be destroyed by each other."

Paul wrote this letter to the Galatian Church about the freedom that Jesus had given them. Paul wanted the Galatians to feel God's sovereignty and to use it wisely. Paul was writing about the churches that were being torn between the old laws (Old Testament) and the grace and mercy of Jesus Christ (New Testament.) Even churches today find it hard to preach one way. One thinks they should use the Old and New Testament, while other churches believe the Old Testament(law) isn't prevalent. The sad part when priests or preachers say something, people will listen. Some don't read parts of the Bible because they are being told this isn't vital. God put all the chapters in the Bible for a reason.

The Old Testament gives us history. We don't want to repeat the same mistakes the Israelites made in the past. The wisdom Solomon wrote about in Proverbs is what we still base our principles around today. Those truths were fundamental yesterday as they are today. The Psalms are an essential part of our worship. The more I study the characters in the Old

Testament, and the more I learn about myself. Scientists have tried to prove Genesis wrong, but they haven't given us an explanation for creation that says God did not create us. Can you imagine how much suffering people could have eliminated by obeying the Ten Commandments?

God, with His infinite knowledge of man, knew we would need something to set us free. God knew how human nature could destroy us. Through history and God's chosen people (Israelites), God knew our human nature could become more important than following His principles. Knowing the law wasn't enough, He sent down His only begotten Son to make atonement for the sins we would commit. Jesus paid the ultimate sacrifice by dying on the cross. Then God could have propitiation (God's favor) to forgive our sins.

John 3:16-17: "For God so loved the world that He gave His one and only Son, that whoever believes in Him shall not perish but have eternal life. For God did not send His Son into the world to condemn the world, but to save the world through Him." By faith, accepting Jesus as my Lord and Savior, I became a part of Jesus' redemption by my willingness to repent; God would forgive my trespasses. Being a part of His salvation set me free.

Romans 5:20-21: "The law was added so that the trespass might increase. But where sin increased, grace increased all the more, so that, just as sin reigned in death, so also grace might reign through righteousness to bring eternal life through Jesus Christ our Lord." The old laws consisted of 700 different rules. Laws governed the Old Testament, but in many cases, sin would increase.

Before Jesus died, sin had reigned because he rose from the dead, His grace and mercy could lead us to righteousness (doing right in the eyes of God), and by His grace, we could have eternal freedom. We are no longer under the law but under God's grace and mercy.

A friend of mine once asked me, "What if heaven doesn't exist?" Then he asked me, "Don't people go to God because they are weak?" Looking at him, I said what was on my heart. I told him my life has gotten so much better since I became a Christian. I have goals; I feel an inner peace I never had before. I don't worry about things that I can't change. I am falling in love with my wife for the right reasons. Jesus has stirred up my passion for new people that I meet. Since I met Jesus, my life has gotten so much better. I no longer stay depressed and feel all alone.

I continued by saying; I went outside this morning and could hear the birds chirping in the air. The sunrise seemed a little brighter. For the first time, I know the meaning of peace.

I looked at my friend again; God has given me a piece of His glory; I can feel His Spirit inside me. "To the Jews who had believed Him, Jesus said, 'If you hold to my teachings, you are really my disciples.' Then you will know the truth, and the truth will set you free (John 8:31-32.)" After quoting that scripture, I ended by saying, "the truth was never a part of my life; following His revelation (Jesus truth) has set me free!"

CHAPTER 3

Jesus Wants to Save Our Souls

The soul of man is eternal. When we die, our physical bodies will turn to dust, but our soul is immortal. What we feel inside, how we treated people who crossed our path, how we valued God, all these things are what lies inside our soul. When we die, God will judge us by what He sees in our souls. I firmly believe how we live our life is preparing us for when we meet our Creator. To think my soul might live inside another body is truly exciting.

John 4:13-15: "Jesus answered, 'Everyone who drinks this water will be thirsty again, but whoever drinks the water I give him will become in him a spring of water welling up to eternal life.' The woman said to Him, 'Sir, give me this water so that I won't get thirsty and have to keep coming here to draw water.'"

Jesus met this woman at the well outside her city, and they started to talk. The woman seemed confused. Maybe no one spoke to her about spiritual things. Spiritual things affect the human spirit or the soul. Jesus spoke to her about her life and some of her past marriages. She thought He was a prophet. Jesus spoke to her about the Samaritans in her town and how they worshiped and how they would worship His Father in spirit one day.

John 4:25-26: "The woman said, I know that Messiah(called Christ) is coming. When He comes, He will explain everything to us. Then Jesus replied, 'I who speak to you am He.'" The disciples came back and saw Jesus talking to the woman. The woman went back to town and told people about the man she met at the well. After learning the man knew everything about her, many people went out to meet Jesus at the well.

Meanwhile, the apostles urged Jesus to eat some food. Even the apostles were not aware of the food(spiritual things); they questioned Him if He had eaten.

John 4:34: "My food, said Jesus is to do the will of Him who sent Me and to finish His work." Then Jesus talks to them about the spiritual harvest. The harvest of people(people the apostles could witness to) people that were ripe and waiting to hear His word.

Going to Church and reading the Bible is essential, but reaching out to people who need God is never finished. We can be Christians in word only, but being a disciple means being God's hands and heart while we are living. Verse 37: "Thus the saying 'One sow and another reaps' is true." Both the sower who does God's work or the person who reaps God's benefits gives them both profit.

If we call ourselves Christian, why do we deprive our souls of living water? Jesus Christ is the living water. His written words are in the Bible. When we read the Bible, His living water can fill our souls; When we perform works of kindness toward others, God is doing His work through us. Living water is thirsting for God as we thirst for water!

Just remember Jesus had to die, then God could send the Holy Spirit down. After being filled with the Holy Spirit, the apostles became sowers and doers of God's harvest. Like the woman at the well, I lived a life opposed to God's will. It wasn't until I met Jesus that my life would change.

Matthew 16:24-25: "Then Jesus said to His disciples, 'If anyone would come after me, he must deny himself and take up his cross and follow Me.' For whoever wants to save his life will lose it, but whoever loses his life for me will find it." Then in verse 26, He asks the apostles and us a question: "What good will it be for a man if he gains the whole world, yet forfeits his soul?"

When we pick up our cross, many of us have to make changes that are a necessary part of being disciples. Jesus wants us to be a part of His journey; by picking up our cross, we are willing to make sacrifices. By picking up our cross and following Him, we become a part of His salvation.

The Holy Spirit would challenge me. When we face those challenges, my soul got stronger. I started giving up doing some things and habits that no longer could fill my soul.

When I started giving up the things that are part of the world, I learned this would help me grow. I had a choice of what I could change. I had the strength to make those changes. I started to feel better about this life and the direction it was going. Jesus gave my soul a voice.

Ephesians 3:14-16: "For this reason, I kneel before the Father, from whom His whole family in heaven and on earth derives its name. I pray that out of His glorious riches, and He may strengthen you with power through His Spirit in your inner being.

Jesus isn't just reaching out to the Ephesians when he speaks these words; he is reaching out to everyone throughout the world. He is praying that out of God's most enormous riches that Jesus and the Holy Spirit can fill the earth. Living a life patterned around the way Jesus lived, you can receive those riches!

In verses 17-19, Paul continues praying: "So that Christ may dwell in your hearts through faith. And I pray that you, being rooted and established in love, may have power, together with all the saints, to grasp how wide and long and high and deep is the love of Christ, and to know this love that surpasses knowledge--that you may be filled to the measure of all the fullness of God."

I didn't deserve the love and mercy God gave me, but He still gave it to me. A miracle began to happen; I began to feel His love inside me.

My knowledge before meeting Jesus only brought me sadness. The love I found in Jesus brought me to the foot of the cross, and I repented. Repentance(feeling sorry and changing) brought me the wisdom that would save my soul.

I pray that whoever we meet will feel the light of God's salvation that will shine through us. I pray I can be a source of peace when I deal with family and friends. I pray for all of God's churches. I pray for our country and our leaders. I pray for all the countries in the world that they may have a revival. That they may feel the love Jesus wants to give them, and that love helps us work together.

Ephesians 3:20-21: "Now to Him who is able to do immeasurably more than all we ask or imagine, according to His power that is at work within us, to Him be glory in the Church and Christ Jesus throughout the generations, forever and ever! Amen."

CHAPTER 4

Press On. Hang in there!

1 Corinthians 2:9-10: "However, as it is written: What no eye has seen, no ear has heard, no mind has conceived-what God has prepared for those who love Him- but God has revealed it to us by His Spirit-The Spirit searches all things, even the deep things of God."

When I first became a Christian, I asked Gavin, "What if heaven doesn't exist?" And if heaven doesn't exist, then the life we are leading has no reward. His answer came quickly, "then this is a great way to live my life."

Gavin is 24 years old, has been to Africa twice, Greenland, and just got back from China. All these were mission trips that he financed with his own money. Gavin has a brain that serves the Lord.

I can honestly say knowing Jesus has exceeded all my expectations, and God has blessed me in many ways. I have watched the people in my Bible study go through so much on their journey; even though they had problems, they would press on. My problems seemed small compared to all the things they were going through. I never heard them complain. They would take the time to answer my question. They would always quote scripture when they gave me an answer. These were people who have studied the Bible for many years.

DO YOU KNOW THE TRUTH?

I would watch Elaine come on her walker, a brace wrapped around her waist. She was so determined to be a part of our Bible study. Her husband had just passed away before I knew her. Her grandson Nathan still lived with her and never married. Both of them are devoted Christians. Harley had a wife that was losing her memory; the love he had for his wife was amazing. Can you imagine a person 92 years old changing his wife's diapers? And if you asked him if it was hard, this was just a normal part of living; Jesus was helping him do what needed doing. To this day, I admire the wisdom God has given him. He knew how to guide a young Christian and keep him from getting frustrated. At that time, three Apostolics, three Pentecostals, and me a member of a Lutheran Church. I think Jesus was pleased that we could all blend as one.

Greg and his family wanted to stay in their home, but Greg wasn't working and needed a job. His faith in Jesus blew me away. Even though he wasn't working at the time, management found a way for him to stay based on his merit. Gordon had been a Christian for many years. He would encourage me to write; many of the papers I would write, he copied and passed them out at his church every Sunday. All these people were part of the puzzle God was putting together. I am so grateful God put these people in my life; I wouldn't be the person I am today without their guidance.

1 Corinthians 9:24-25: "Do you not know that in a race all the runners run, but only one gets the prize? Run in such a way as to get the prize. Everyone who competes in the games goes into strict training. They do it to get a crown that will not last, but we do it to get a crown that will last forever."

There is a formula for the Christian life that can lead to success, obedience + commitment = discipline. By training every day, we develop discipline. We have a daily reprieve on our journey. We are a Christian in word only doesn't amount to growth. If we want to be a disciple, then we become a part of Jesus and His purpose. His Spirit can work through us;

we help people who need God's help. We plant seeds along our path that can draw people closer to God. There was a constant theme in what Paul would write to the churches. The need to run the race, press on, and go into training was a life that would lead us toward discipline.

Despite the obstacles, we press on. There will be times when we are sick. When our loved ones don't want our guidance, Satan will attack any weakness in our Spirit. Regardless of the struggles, Paul is encouraging us to press on. We will fail at times, but God's forgiveness is always there to comfort us. Finding a good church, reading the Bible every day, and getting around other Christians helps us stay in training. Doing these things will keep you grounded.

Philippians 3:12-14: "Not that I have already obtained all this, or have already arrived at my goal, but I press on to take hold of that for which Christ Jesus took hold of me. Brothers and sisters, I do not consider myself yet to have taken hold of it. But one thing I do: Forgetting what is behind and straining toward what is ahead. I press on toward the goal to win the prize for which God has called me heavenward in Christ Jesus." Paul's goal meant spending his eternity with Jesus.

Paul watched so many people die because they called themselves Christians. God had forgiven him for all the sins he committed in his past life. Paul was put in jail several times and beaten, but Jesus gave him the strength to write 30 percent of the New Testament. Here is a man who worked harder than all the apostles, suffered immensely but had the humility to admit he didn't know it all. His letters to the churches continue to encourage billions of people to press on.

We know Paul had many obstacles, but he never quit trying to serve God's purpose. In our lifetime, we will have trials, times when God seems far away, but we continue to press on. Things in this world will happen(sickness, tragedies, grief), keeping our focus on God; we still push forward. Like Paul, I don't know it all, I don't have all the answers, but regardless of the obstacles in my path, I press forward!

CHAPTER 5

The Answer: It Starts With Me

I was in a fog for most of my life. I was blind; I couldn't see how depression was tearing me apart. After making Jesus my Lord and Savior, I talked to a Christian friend about some of my problems. He asked me if I read the Bible, then he told me if I start reading the Bible, I will get some answers.

In my mind, the problem was ever one else, if only they could change. Here I am on the verge of another divorce. I was watching my life fall apart and not being able to stop the downward cycle. Let me repeat it, "If only everyone else could change, I wouldn't have any of these problems!" When Jesus walked the earth, He set an example for us to follow. Was I ready to follow His example?

The next day I picked up that Bible gathering dust and started reading the Book of Matthew. I learned about Jesus' birth and how God sent Him down to save us from ourselves. Looking back, why did it take so long for me to admit defeat? Here I am, sixty years old, and finally, after all these years, I started listening to what God had to say.

I grew up in a Catholic Church, and my parents sent me there to school. I attended Mass almost every day, but I did all these things in a fog. It wasn't God's fault; I really can't blame the Catholic Church. I am glad my parents give me a foundation that kept me out of trouble until I got older. I don't think schools back then could handle depressed kids. Many of those good kids, the quiet and obedient kids, are sad (discouraged) and needed help!

Matthew 11:28-30: "Come to me, all you who are weary and burdened, and I will give you rest. Take my yoke upon you and learn from Me, for I am gentle and humble in heart, and you will find rest for your souls. For My yoke is easy and My burden is light."

I was weary and tired. I think reading the Bible that first morning put my soul at rest. I was tired of running and having to start over, and for the first time in a long time, I was willing to listen.

Something inside me kept me reading. Instead of worrying, I began to feel hope. When I started to learn about Jesus and how He paid the ultimate sacrifice for the sins I committed, forgiveness took on a greater meaning. I was fighting with the past, and all the guilt was tearing me apart. At that moment, I asked God for His forgiveness.

I was attending church; the sermons took on a definite meaning. I remember listening to the Pastor talk about Genesis and creation, and I realized God created us in His image. I heard this message preached throughout my life, but I listened to what God told me for the first time in my life. I started reading the Bible every day; my friend and I started a Bible study group in our neighborhood; all these things took on a greater meaning and gave my life purpose. It wasn't my nature to do these things, but God was leading me to do them!

Matthew 10: 37-39: "Anyone who loves his father or mother more than Me is not worthy of Me; anyone who loves his son or daughter more than Me is not worthy of Me. Whoever does not take up his cross and follow Me is not worthy of Me. Whoever finds his life will lose it, and whoever loses his life for My sake will find it."

Before any good could happen, I had to keep God first in my life. Making God first in my life would benefit my family in many ways. What does it mean to carry my cross? It means I was willing to change, through prayer and meditation, including God in all my decisions. I went to God, hoping He could save my marriage, but I got so much more than what I wanted. I got a Savior who was changing me into a better person.

Matthew 11:27: "All things have been committed to Me by my Father. No one knows the Son except the Father, and no one knows the Father except the Son and those to whom the Son chooses to reveal him."

For you to know God and His will, you need to have an intimate relationship with Jesus. The people who accept Jesus as their Lord and Savior become a member of God's family. We become His children. With child-like faith, we put our trust in God, and He begins to teach us His ways.

Matthew 13:31-32: "He told them another parable: 'The kingdom of heaven is like a mustard seed, which a man took and planted in his kingdom. Though it is the smallest of all your seeds, yet when it grows, it is the largest of garden plants and becomes a tree so that the birds of the air come and perch in its branches." Just like a mustard seed grows, so will our faith. Even when times seemed hard, God would work things out. By putting my trust in someone other than myself, my life started to produce some good results. I often tell people who have struggles don't quit before the miracle happens. It takes time for faith to develop, take the time to let it happen!

Romans 12:1-2: "Therefore I urge you, brothers, in view of God's mercy, to offer your bodies as living sacrifices, holy and pleasing to God-- this is your spiritual act of worship. Do not conform any longer to the pattern of the world, but be transformed by the renewing of your mind. Then you will be able to test and approve what God's will is-His good pleasing and perfect will."

I started to pray and include God in all my decisions. God would fill my Spirit with what I needed. A miracle began to happen; The Holy Spirit began to transform me into a different person. The barriers that were hurting me in the past would start to fade away. The fog (depression) started to lift.

I study the Bible. I try doing the will of God in all my affairs. I no longer wanted the people in my life to change; I knew the change would come through the Spirit that was filling my soul. I knew it was God's place to change my loved ones. The more dependence I put on God, the more peace I would feel.

I think my whole life I spent looking toward people to give me validation (acceptance), now doing what was right in God's eyes, gave me what I needed. Struggles became a way of learning about what I needed to change. For the first time in a long time, Jesus was helping me find some answers!

CHAPTER 6

The Answer to Sin: The Answer Lies in Saying No

Matthew 6:33: "But seek first His kingdom and His righteousness, and all these things will be given to you as well." Jesus says to make Him a priority by seeking and striving to do His will; His righteousness can become a part of our soul. One of the things that will happen is that we will have an answer and the ability to combat any sin that comes into our lives.

When I started studying sin and how God had an answer that could lead to eternal freedom, four things became apparent. The first was having a willingness inside my heart that would allow my mind to change. What will be given to you if you seek out His righteousness as a desire to change? Being reasonable means doing what is morally right in the eyes of God; Do I have a willingness to do what is right?

The second part of wanting His righteousness has humility. If I am humble, the Holy Spirit will show me what I need to change. It became a question of who I could change (myself) and what kept me from doing the will of God. Digging inside myself, I thought, "I'm giving up doing things I truly enjoy." I realized God wanted to give me the things I needed, and how God could fill those needs would develop character. By building character, God could make me stronger. God wasn't telling me to give up the things I enjoyed, but some of the things I enjoyed doing were keeping my spirit in bondage.

John 3:7-8: "You should not be surprised at my saying, 'You must be born again.' The wind blows wherever it pleases. You hear its sound, but you can not tell where it comes from or where it is going. So it is with everyone born of the Spirit." Was Jesus telling me, "You must be born of the Spirit?" There are two births, and does our second birth make a difference in our Christian life?

The third thing began to happen; after I started speaking in tongues, I knew something changed inside me. It wasn't a language I was saying, but the Holy Spirit was speaking through me. The moment that happened, I felt different. I knew my life was going to change.

John 3:16-17: "For God so loved the world that He gave His one and only Son that whoever believes in Him shall not perish but have eternal life. For God did not send His Son into the world to condemn the world, but to save the world through Him." Jesus didn't come down to condemn. He wanted to save us from ourselves.

Proverbs 11:2: "When pride comes, then comes disgrace, but with humility comes wisdom." My pride says, "You are growing in the right direction." Satisfaction says, "I have grown in all the areas that needed growth, isn't that enough." Humility says, "Do you want to remove the areas in your life that will only lead to pain?" Humility says, "Do you want to become the person worthy to meet your Creator?" The Holy Spirit is always showing me areas that need improvement.

Proverbs 11:4: "Wealth is worthless in the days of wrath, but righteousness delivers from death." Wealth or what I thought could make me happy all those things are worthless on judgment day. What do I consider important? What do we strive to achieve in our personal lives?

How we live our life, what we have done for others, this is what God sees. Did I serve His purpose when called to serve? God will look at our soul and the way we lived.

The fourth thing I had to look at was temptation. Satan is trying to find ways to weaken the Holy Spirit inside you. Learning to handle temptation can lead to our faith getting stronger (conviction.)

Matthew 4:5-6: "Then the devil took Him to the holy city and had Him stand on the highest point of the temple. 'If you are the Son of God,' he said, throw yourself down. For it is written: 'He will command His angels concerning You, and they will lift You up in their hands so that You will not strike your foot against a stone.'"

Satan wants to taunt you and make you feel what he is telling you is correct. He gives us justification for doing the wrong things! God put beautiful people before us, so we should admire their beauty? Does admiring their beauty lead to sin?

Verse 7: Jesus answered him, "It is also written: 'Do not put your God to the test.'" When we get tempted, I resist Satan by saying no!

James 1:13-15: "When tempted, no one should say, 'God is tempting me.' For God cannot be tempted by evil, nor does He tempt anyone; but each one is tempted when, by his own evil desire, he is dragged away and enticed. Then. after desire is conceived, it gives birth to sin; and sin, when it is full-grown, gives birth to death." Being human at times, we will fail, but we give birth to an end when we willingly sin. Unless I work in those areas, they won't improve. God knows that we will fail; I learned to measure growth, not by counting how many times I sinned; I measure growth by the progress I have made.

We did a Bible study on "Guardrails." Andy Stanley wrote this book. According to Andy, "guardrail is a standard of behavior that becomes a matter of conscience." Our conscience dictates to us what is right and wrong. When we see guardrails, we stop, knowing it will lead to sin. I am learning to stop when I come to a guardrail and listen to what my conscience is telling me.

Changing isn't easy, but failing to try only leads our soul in the wrong direction. There are times in our Christian lives that we need to make choices. The decisions we make can lead to real change. Take the time to realize how temptation caused you so much pain.

There are seven deadly sins: lust, gluttony, greed, sloth, wrath, envy, and pride. God had intended purposes for sex, food, and money. Laziness, anger, jealousy, and pride can destroy the Spirit that lives inside us. If I am not aware of the seven deadly sins, they can creep into my life.

Ephesians 5:17: "Therefore do not be foolish, but understand what the Lord's will is." Every decision we make affects ourselves and the people around us. It comes down to following the path that leads to eternal freedom. I need to keep doing the things that keep me focused on God. The answer to sin truly lies in us, saying no! It depends on how strong God's Spirit is working through you. The more we say "no," the more Satan loses his power!

CHAPTER 7

Anger: What God Says About Anger

Anger can destroy your life and the lives of your loved ones. Anger can rob us of the joy God has given us. Anger can ruin all good things God has accomplished in our lives. Satan uses rage to keep us from the victories God wants in our life. I have found that anger is the worst enemy anyone can carry around.

If our motives are selfish and things don't go our way, we get angry. If we get jealous or our feelings get hurt, our anger can arise. Maybe we deserve advance at work, and someone less worthy gets promoted; these are reasons why anger can turn to violence. Even if God doesn't answer our prayers, there are so many reasons we can get angry. What many people don't realize anger puts judgment on us.

Psalms 37:8-9: "Refrain from anger, and turn from wrath; do not fret--it leads only to evil. For evil men will get cut off, but those who hope in the LORD will inherit the land."

If we have an impulse to react when we are angry, God wants us to refrain. Instead of going off in a rage or getting angrier, God wants us to turn away from the wrath we are feeling. Instead of holding on to the anger, Jesus teaches us to let go. Jesus shows us how to handle anger; by the way, He lived His life. If we want to live in God's land and inherit His blessings, then we will learn how to manage our anger.

In Psalm 37: David is giving us a contrast between a righteous man and an evil man. The honest man tries to do good in the eyes of God, while the wicked man tries to handle things his way. The righteous man refrains from getting angry, while the evil man allows his anger to get out of control.

There is something that happens to me when I hold on to anger. Anger turns to resentment, and resentment turns into self-pity. The self-pity keeps me blocked out from the love and comfort God can give me. Anger robs me of the joy inside me, it can keep me isolated and depressed, and for some, their anger lasts a lifetime.

Genesis 4:11-15, we learn about Cain and Abel. Cain's jealousy caused him to kill his brother. Genesis 27:41 tells us the story of Jacob tricking his father. Esau, who was the oldest son, lost all his birthrights. Esau spent a short lifetime (twenty years) being angry and seeking revenge against his brother.

Jonah got mad at God for not destroying the people of Nineveh. God wanted him to go on a mission and save those people; instead, he rebelled against God's will and ran. He ended up on a boat, jumping off the ship, but God didn't want him to die. A big fish came up and swallowed him.

What is important is the lessons we learn from many of the stories we read about in the Bible. The great fish in this story symbolizes how our anger can swallow us up and keep us isolated.

When people hurt us, forgiveness gives us the freedom to move on. We might get angry for a while, but that anger doesn't keep us from moving forward; the offense will keep us isolated.

Matthew 5:21-22: "You have heard that it was said to the people long ago, 'Do not murder,' and anyone who murders will be subject to judgment. But I tell you that anyone angry with his brother will be subject to judgment." Jesus compares unforgiveness to murder; by being angry, we pass judgment on ourselves. God wants us to realize that staying angry can hurt us.

Matthew 5:38-39: "You have heard that it said, 'Eye for eye, and a tooth for a tooth.' But I tell you. Do not resist an evil person. If someone strikes you on the right cheek, turn to him the other also." Jesus is talking about retaliation. Nowhere in the New Testament does it talk about getting even. Jesus doesn't want us to use our anger in the wrong way.

While walking on the earth, Jesus endured insult after insult. Regardless of the hatred around Him, He didn't avoid being around the evil people. Regardless of the lies spread about Him, even the blows He received while dying, He would turn the other cheek. Words spoken while He was on the cross, "Father forgive them, they know not what they do."

Some people are blind when it comes to forgiveness; do we pass judgment, or do we forgive them? Do we show them the same mercy that Jesus shows us? If we are committed to the Lord, we will find it in our hearts to get along with everyone.

Matthew 5:43-44: "You have heard it was said, 'Love your neighbor and hate your enemy.' But I tell you: "Love your enemies and pray for those who persecute you, that you may be sons of your Father in heaven."

Jesus is telling us to love our enemies. The opposite of getting angry is by loving them. Praying for them is a way of leading our Spirit toward forgiveness. Even if we don't like someone, we can be kind and loving toward them.

James 1:19-20: "My dear brothers, take note of this: Everyone should be quick to listen, slow to speak and slow to become angry, for man's anger does not bring about the righteous life God desires."

If we are quick to listen to the words Jesus is telling us, "We won't be so quick to get angry." I meditate and study the Bible every morning. By praying, the Holy Spirit gives me a course of action that will lead to righteousness. Righteousness means following my conscience and doing what is right in the eyes of God.

People use the phrase, "Silence is golden." When dealing with hurt feelings, isn't being silent better than overreacting and saying things you might regret? Isn't being silent and talking to God better than being angry? God wants us to think before we react!

When I started to read the New Testament, I thought God does things the opposite of how the world does. Jesus talks about forgiveness, loving your enemies, and treating people with kindness; this was how He lived. Jesus knew anger could destroy any hope he had of being productive.

Ephesians 4:26-27: "In your anger, do not sin. Do not let the sun go down while you are still angry, and do not give the devil a foothold." I will get hurt, but anger can no longer destroy the life God is building up in me.

How many married couples go to bed angry at each other. Waking up the following day, still upset, then we say things meant to hurt each other. The reason many fights continue is no one wants to admit they are wrong.

Philippians 2:3-4: "Do nothing out of selfish ambition or vain conceit, but in humility, consider others better than yourselves. Each of you should look not only to your interests but also to the interests of others." Paul wrote letters to different churches while being persecuted and put into prison. The world says, "He had every right to get angry." Paul knew anger would only destroy him. Instead of getting angry, God used his situation in the right way; while in prison, he wrote thirty percent of the New Testament!

In a small Mississippi town, a gunman went in and started shooting. People lost their lives; they never found out why the killer went in and started shooting. Shortly after this happened, the church members came out and publicly forgave him.

They were not saying what he did was right; it wasn't! Instead of being angry and wanting revenge, they forgave him. They were free to bury their loved ones (mourn) and move forward. They set an example for all of us to follow. If any good came out of this tragedy, it was the forgiveness that helped them to move forward. They set an example for all of us to follow!

CHAPTER 8

Believers, Doubters, Mockers

John 20:21-22: "Again Jesus said, 'Peace be with you! As the Father has sent Me. I am sending you.' And with that, He breathed on them and said, 'Receive the Holy Spirit.'"

After rising from the dead, Jesus appeared to the apostles behind locked doors. In that room, He breathed on them, and they were filled with the Holy Spirit. From the moment that happened, their lives changed!

Acts 2:1-3: "When the day of Pentecost came, they were all together in one place. Suddenly a sound like the blowing of a violent wind came from heaven and filled the whole house where they were sitting. They saw what seemed to be tongues of fire that separated and came to rest on each of them."

Before I go any farther, there are entire books written on the Book of Acts. To fully understand what happened, you need to read the whole chapter. The gentile talked about in many verses are the non-jews. Even today, the Jews still believe in the Old Testament and the laws written years ago. With the birth and crucifixion of Jesus, we no longer are under the law but God's grace and mercy. Pentecost was also called the Feast of Weeks. People gathered annually in Jerusalem and had a festival of thanksgiving for the harvested crops.

Verses 5-6: "Now there was staying in Jerusalem God-fearing Jews from every nation under heaven. When they heard this sound, a crowd came together in bewilderment, because each one heard them speaking in his language." This group was called the doubters. They saw people speaking in their tongues, but they didn't know what was happening to them. Even in churches today where people worship and pray in the Spirit, people are skeptical. It's hard for them to believe that God can exist in all the koas!

On this day of Pentecost, God poured out His Spirit. Verses 10-11: "Phrygia and Pamphylia, Egypt and parts of Libia near Cyrene; visitors from Rome (both Jews and converts to Judaism); Cretans and Arabs---we hear them declaring the wonders of God in our own tongues!" All of them were amazed and perplexed. Verse 13: "Some, however, made fun of them and said, 'They have had too much wine.'" These people are called the mockers.

Peter, who denied Jesus three times, would address the crowd. Peter, filled with the Holy Spirit, became bold, more Spirit-filled. Peter was addressing the group and telling them about Jesus. He reminded the mockers that it was only nine o'clock in the morning. Peter told them about Joel's prophesy, Jesus, coming back in the final days, how God would pour out His Spirit in those days. He reminded them how they worked with wicked men, put Jesus on the cross, and crucified Him.

When the people heard this, they were cut to the heart and said to Peter and the other apostles, "Brothers, what shall we do?" In verses 38-39, Peter replied, "Repent and be baptized, every one of you, in the name of Jesus Christ for the forgiveness of your sins. And you will receive the Gift of the Holy Spirit. The promise is for you and your children and for all who are far off--for all whom the Lord will call." When called, we repent and ask God for forgiveness; you become a believer. Shortly afterward, you will receive the baptism of the Holy Spirit.

In acts chapter 9, we learn about (Saul) Paul's conversion. As he neared Damascus on his journey, suddenly a light flashed around him.

He fell to the ground and heard a voice say to him, 'Saul, Saul, why do you persecute Me?' 'Who are you, Lord?' Saul asked." Saul went to great lengths to persecute Christians. He would travel hundreds of miles, find Christians put them in chains, and drag them back to Jerusalem. But God had another purpose for Paul(called) and stopped him on his journey to Damascus. The men traveling with Paul were speechless, seeing that he was blind, they led him by foot into Damascus.

In Damascus, there was a man named Ananias. The Lord called on Ananias in a vision. God told him to go to a house where Paul was staying. He was to place hands on Paul's eyes, and he would see.

Acts 9:15-16: "But the Lord said to Ananias, Go! This man is my chosen instrument to carry My name before the Gentiles and their kings, and before the people of Israel. I will show him how much he must suffer for my name." Despite the fear Ananias was feeling, God's fear was more potent, and he went to the house where Paul was staying.

Paul suffered almost daily after being filled with the Holy Spirit. He was transformed from a man who persecuted Christians into a man who would die for Jesus Christ! While in prison, he would write letters to the different churches. Paul's testimony would touch the lives of non-believers (Gentiles)and give everyone the ability to follow Jesus. When we read his letters, they encourage and teach us. When we study his letters, we see weaknesses even in our churches today.

You will find the believers who were filled with the Holy Spirit and spoke in different tongues throughout history. They are filled with the Holy Spirit and begin to do amazing things. There will always be the doubters, people on the fence looking at us with bewilderment. These people watch Spirit-filled Christians going about and accomplishing great things, but they seem content staying in their place of comfort. Even the apostles who were part of Jesus' journey at times were doubtful and lacking in faith.

We are fortunate in our country that we have the freedom to believe in God; many nations and fellow Christians in the world are under persecution because of their beliefs. Some people are still being targeted because they are Christians(isis.) My friend was put in jail, trying to bring Bibles into Korea. Jesus Christ wants to help everyone globally; because people doubt, God can't reach them. Jesus knows who will accept Him, so He waits patiently for the right time to come into their lives.

Then comes the mockers, people who criticize, people who ridicule the word of God, and refuse to believe. Throughout history, we have the mockers.

Nehemiah 4:1-2: "When Sanballat heard that Nehemiah and the Israelites were rebuilding the wall, he became angry and was greatly incensed. He ridiculed the Jews, and in the presence of his associates and the army of Samaria, he said, 'What are these feeble Jews doing?' Will they restore their wall? Will they offer sacrifices? Will they finish in a day? 'Can they bring the stones back to life from those heaps of rubble--burned as they are?"

Sanballat was governor of Samaria, the region just north of Judea. God appointed Nehemiah to go and rebuild the walls of Jerusalem. Sanballat, because of his ridicule, only caused hatred and separation between the people. The Jews and Samaritans ended up hating each other.

Despite the mockers, Nehemiah, through prayer and following God's will---rebuild the wall. Nehemiah was a leader; he could organize, and with God's help, unite the people. God used Nehemiah to serve His purpose. God uses people who He knows will serve His purpose. Then He gives them the power to carry out His mission. God puts people in our path that we are capable of helping.

Even on our Christian journey, we will face the mockers; we will face skepticism from some people that cross our path. The Holy Spirit is more reliable than the doubts of people who cross our path!

Matthew 27: 30-31: "They spit on Him, and took the staff and struck Him on the head again and again. After they mocked Him, they took off the robe and put His own clothes on Him. Then they led Him away to crucify Him."

Despite the mockers, Jesus moved on and did what God called him to do. Some people will criticize our efforts. Some people doubt the existence of God and refuse to let Him into their lives. Some people will call you Holy-roller or a fanatic, but no one can take God's Spirit away from the true believer!

CHAPTER 9

Being Critical

How we act and the kindness we show others are ways God uses us to plant seeds. Being high on life one day and the doomsayer the next won't help winning souls over to God. I want to present a Spirit that people can build their trust around. I can't introduce myself as joyous and accessible, and the next day, I am angry and critical. The world will judge me by how we conduct ourselves. Being judgmental and vital tells the people around us; you're not good enough.

Matthew 7:1-3: "Do not judge, or you too will be judged. For the same way you judge others, you will be judged, and with the measure you use, it will be measured to you. Why do you look at the speck of sawdust in your brother's eye and pay no attention to the plank in your eye?"

I don't know what another person has gone through unless I get to know them. The easy thing for me is to judge people by the way they look and act; being a part of Jesus' salvation teaches me how to understand others before I decide. If I am judgmental, I can't hear what they are saying.

Before I made Jesus a part of my life, I was no better than the lost soul walking down the street. Despite all my character defects, Jesus accepted me. God wants us to have the same understanding toward others as He had toward us. Part of the plank in my eye can be judging others. Another plank is judging others, so I don't have to look at myself.

Matthew 7:4: "How can you say to your brother, 'Let me take the speck out of your eye when all the time there is a plank in your eye.'" The plank in your eye is your judgment. We are not on this earth to judge people. It's our goal to win souls and plant seeds that can grow.

Verse 5: "You hypocrite, first take the plank out of your own eye, and then you will see clearly to remove the speck from your brother's eye." When I point the finger at someone else, even my loved ones, the other four fingers point back to me. Before judgment leads to my criticism, I need to pause before saying something that will hurt them.

Even in our homes, if we want to be effective, we allow our loved ones to speak. Always having the last word shows them we aren't listening to what they are saying. A big part of helping people isn't by fixing them. Many times they need to be heard; friendship is a big part of introducing them to Jesus.

When I wrote the book "It Starts With Me," just that admission made a difference in my life. When I criticize a loved one, it leads to them feeling not validated. By having the last word, their opinions don't matter. If we are critical of our children, it will hinder their ability to grow. Why try doing different things if we are always criticized for doing them? Taking time to listen and meditating on how we can help them leads to progress. The best way I can help anyone is by setting a good example.

Proverbs 9:8: "Do not rebuke a mocker or he will hate you; rebuke a wise man, and he will love you." The mocker is critical, while the wise man listens, learns, and even when criticized, is thankful. Not everyone is capable of hearing what you have to say. If I am humble, even when attacked, I will listen and learn.

We can't win the love and respect of others until I get to know them. I can't become the person God wants me to be unless my inner feelings get out of the way. If I am critical, it usually means something is going on inside of me. God helped me see that I need to look inward when I am dangerous (critical) before I minister to others' needs.

Do I want to help people? Yes, I do! Before that can happen, It has to start with me. When I quit pointing the finger, God can show me how I can help. I want people to come to me, not to turn the other way when they see me coming. Even loved ones can be more accepting and trusting because of the changes we have made. Instead of arguing or trying to change them, we can plant some seeds when we listen.

We are here on earth for a short while. We need to ask ourselves, "Am I growing and changing into the person worthy of calling myself a disciple. Am I less selfish and think of other people more than myself? Is God giving me the understanding I need to help people?

Luke 6:37-38: "Do not judge, and you will not be judged. Do not condemn, and you will not be condemned. Forgive, and you will be forgiven, Give, and it will be given to you. A good measure, pressed down, shaken together and running over, will be poured into your lap. For with the measure you use, it will be measured to you." Jesus uses how they measure grain in a bushel to measure the way we treat others.

With the same measure I use toward others; If I am forgiving, God will forgive me, but God will judge my behavior when I am judgmental. God is using a paradox in the verses above so that He can get His message across. Everyone deserves to know about God's salvation, but how we do that is important.

How I treat others shows them I care. God gives us so much, and the more we give to others, the more He gives us. When I am critical and not showing people the love God has given me, God will keep His love from me!

CHAPTER 10

Bible Studies

1 Samuel 23:16: "And Saul's son Johnathan went to David at Horesh and helped him find strength in God." Saul was jealous of David; he went to any lengths trying to kill him. God would send Saul's son to give David a message. Verse 17: "Don't be afraid, he said, 'My father Saul will not lay a hand on you.' You will be King over Israel, and I will be second to you. Even my father knows this."

I like to think our Bible studies are a way of God giving us answers. When I go to my Bible studies, it helps me stay connected to God. When I have problems, there is support and comfort. Proverbs 27:17: "As iron sharpens iron, so one man sharpens another." God doesn't want us to isolate and try solving problems by ourselves. There is a sharpness that comes around when two or more gather.

Hebrews 10:24-25: "And let us consider how we may spur one another on toward love and good deeds. Let us not give up meeting together, as some are in the habit of doing, but let us encourage one another--and all the more as you see the day approaching." Paul knew the day was coming when Jesus would come a second time. He knew people would experience persecution and isolation. Back then, they had house churches. They could gather and give each other support.

DO YOU KNOW THE TRUTH?

Bible studies are an essential part of how people can get to know and help you. When we share our problems and doubts with fellow Christians, we gain a better perspective of how God can help us. God wants us to challenge our leaders. What better place to do that but at our Bible Studies?

There are different types of Bible Studies: One where we listen and watch a video and then ask questions. The other is a group of people who meet weekly, usually smaller groups. The church I attend has a Bible study for the woman; after listening to a speaker who gives the study, they break up and go into smaller groups.

After I became a Christian, my friend and I started a Bible study in our neighborhood. It grew to about ten people at times, to a current four or six of us that meet every Monday. There are over 100 years of experience (studying the Bible) in our group. Because of their knowledge and experience, I have learned a lot. In a chapter I wrote earlier, I spoke to you about the members that attend our group. All of them have a broad knowledge of the Bible. I have learned so much from their experience. I wouldn't be able to write books without their inputs.

I also go to a Bible study on Thursday nights. This group is smaller; four of us attend this group regularly. All of us are somewhat busy, but we make it a point to meet a couple of times a month. Paul just retired and travels, Herb just sold his condo, and he and his wife continually travel in their RV. Harold closed on a business and has started another one. Then there is me, and I usually bring along some drama. About a year ago, Paul invited Jim to become a part of our group. Jim was going through cancer.

When I look at the overall picture, we needed each other. Paul just retired, Herb, who was in his seventies and selling their home, even Harold and some of the problems closing down his old business, and me dealing with a son who didn't want my help regardless of all the help he needed.

Paul had some insight into what we all needed because he brought in the material; we all needed to study. The series he brought us to learn was on Psalms 23. At this stage in our lives, all of us were going through change, so God gave us what we needed. I have learned God doesn't always give us what we want, but he always answers our prayers by giving us what we need.

All of us knew that only God could give us comfort and strength when going through our challenges. Studying Psalm 23 gave us the power as we moved through the problems we were all facing.

It's times like this that I realize God shows up when needed. We have faith in a God who is always there when we need comfort and strength. God had His purpose in mind by putting us all together. He knew we would have challenges in our life, and he could lend emotional strength with this group's support.

Watching people stand up in their lives and making changes helped my faith in God grow. Jim never complained about being sick. He continued making plans for the future regardless of cancer. Cancer never beats Jim; I learned you fight cancer by not quitting!

Being there for Jim and the advice he gave me helped me in many ways. Jim gave us more than we could give him. I only hope if ever I have severe sickness that could end my life, I handle it the way Jim did. Because of our busy schedules, we met nineteen times. The church closed through the summer months, so we would gather at Jim's house if he wasn't too sick. Two weeks after the last time we met, Jim passed away!

I am still in awe of how many people were at the service. Jim never talked about his accomplishments and all the things he did for our church. We never knew how many lives he touched. At his funeral, I never saw so many people attend and show respect toward a man and his family. He touched the lives of so many people.

Psalms 23:1: "The Lord is my Shepherd, I shall not be in want." The Lord is our Shepherd. Being our Shepherd, God was giving all of us what we needed. Jesus was guiding all of us into still waters. We were all making decisions in our life that required faith in God. His strength would lead our lives to still waters(making the right decisions.) God showed up and pulled us all together. I remember one of the things Jim told us, "I never feel closer to God than I have while going through cancer." Jim was never a victim but a survivor!

Jim was in the valley when we met Him, but now he is on the upward climb. What a blessing we all received. Paul is a good leader; he continues to bring in material that helps us grow.

We pray together, share our problems; we show God that He is worth our time. We discuss scripture and how we use God for help in our daily lives. Attending my Bible studies has blessed me in many ways. Bible studies are a vital part of keeping us grounded.

CHAPTER 11

Challenges

We might lose a job, or your spouse wants a separation. Maybe we get hurt in a car accident. As grandparents, we have to watch our grandchildren. We have a boss at work, and whatever we do isn't good enough. You are sick, and your life comes to a sudden stop. All these situations above have their challenges. Even though God is a big part of our life, we will still have problems.

Joshua 1:1-2: "After the death of Moses, the servant of the LORD, the LORD said to Joshua son of Nun, Moses aide: Moses, my servant is dead. Now then, you and all these people. get ready to cross the Jordan river into the land I am about to give to them--to the Israelites."

Can you imagine what Joshua felt, losing Moses and having to lead two million people? God wanted Joshua to guide His people into the promised land. Look at how God tested Abraham and how He wanted Abraham to offer up his son as a sacrifice to the LORD. Job when he was going through all his suffering. The only thing that separated these people from others was their faith in God and the ability God gave them to face their challenges.

Paul went from persecuting Christians to accepting Jesus as His Lord and Savior. He was put in chains, whipped several times, put in prison, but he faced those challenges. Steven was one of the first martyrs to die because of his beliefs and willingness to voice them publicly. They would meet their challenges and set an example for all of us to follow.

I Corinthians 9:24-25: "Do you not know that in a race all the runners run, but only one gets the prize? Run in such a way as to get the prize. Everyone who competes in the games goes into strict training. They do it to get a crown that does not last; but we do it to get a crown that lasts forever." Paul knew we would have to face challenges. He compares our journey to a runner who is running a race.

Philippians 3: 12-14: "Not that I have already obtained all this, or have already been made perfect. I press on to take hold of that for which Christ Jesus took hold of me. Brothers, I do not consider myself yet to have taken hold of it. But one thing I do; Forgetting what is behind, and straining for what is ahead." Paul was showing us the meaning of humility (not having all the answers.) The challenge was keeping his eyes on the goal. Instead of Paul getting angry and depressed, he used this time to encourage us.

Verse 14: "I press on toward the goal to win the prize for which God has called me heavenward in Christ Jesus." Paul knew everything he was going through was temporary compared to living a life with Jesus that would last an eternity.

Fighting challenges alone only makes it harder to face. In many cases doing things on my own only made things worst. I had to learn that God could help me, but I had to let Him in!

I had two heart attacks; it was only by God's grace that I might be alive. After the second heart attack, I drove over five miles before reaching the hospital. I remember the last thing before passing out was the nurse telling the doctor; I was dropping down to 15 on my heartbeat. I think I was close to dying. One of the main arteries going into my heart was 100 percent blocked. If I wasn't in the hospital, I would have died!

God wants to be part of our challenges. I lived; my faith in Him got stronger! When my body shuts down, it's time for me to look at life and try making changes that will lead to eternal freedom. It's times like this when God gives us choices on some of the changes I need to make. The challenge becomes, "Do I listen and make those changes?"

I started studying challenges; I realized three things. The first is I know God wants to be part of my problems. Second, am I willing to listen? Third, do I have enough faith in God to make those changes?

John 8:45-47: "Yet because I tell the truth, you do not believe Me! Can any of you prove Me guilty of sin? If I am telling the truth, why don't you believe Me? He who belongs to God hears what God says. The reason you do not hear is that you do not belong to God."

If I listen to God's word and believe the truth will always set me free, do I make excuses to avoid the fact? When faced with challenges, do I follow God's Spirit inside me, telling me what I should do? Let me repeat it, "What I should do!" Going back to the scripture above, am I following Jesus and doing what I need to do?

When Jesus talks about the children of God or belonging to God, He talks to us about the people who have faith in Him. The ones who do things God's way. In the verses above, God is challenging us to find fault in what He is saying. Can we find anything in God's character sinful? In times of need, has He ever failed to give you His love and comfort? When faced with challenges, God wants to help us. When we do the right thing, it will always lead to God and his blessings. We "belong to God" by the way we conduct all our affairs.

2 Peter 3:17-18: "Therefore, dear friends, since you already know this, be on guard so that you may not be carried away by the error of lawless men and fall from a secure position. But grow in grace and knowledge of our Lord and Savior Jesus Christ. To Him be glory both now and forever! Amen."

God is giving His people a challenge; have faith in Me! Don't believe lawless men and some of the things that give us different meanings of God's truth. The challenge to our character is living and doing the will of God in all our affairs. Jesus wants us to stay secure in His word. Do not fall into the world's ways of doing things. Grow in God's knowledge, and His grace will help and carry you.

The challenge is having faith in Him and how he wants to help us. Problems will always be a part of our world; gaining victory over those challenges depends on our attitude and trust (faith) in God. I can't imagine how complex my problems would be; if I had to face them alone!

Circle of Healing

My wife had a daughter who passed away. This daughter was the one I wrote about in the gift. Her name was Trinity, and she was 24 years old when she passed away. This morning September 4, marked the day she died. It was five years ago when she died. Most of our talks on this day would end up with hurt feelings. Three years before we got together, my wife lost Erick in a car accident. Erick was only 21 years old.

It took almost five years before we could talk about Trinity. Today was an answer to prayer. My wife started to talk about all the good memories she had about Trinity, and I could share the things she did that touched my heart. After I became a Christian, I could look back and see Trinity in a different light. Her death was one of the reasons that would lead me to Jesus. In the long run, our marriage would get stronger.

Being able to talk about our feelings would bring God and our marriage closer. It took prayer and patience before the circle of healing happened. I knew how a sudden death in the family could destroy a marriage. The Holy Spirit taught me the meaning of setting boundaries.

When I started to read the gospels: Matthew, Mark, Luke, and John. These books gave me a record of the life of Jesus and some of the miracles He performed. The only way Jesus could prove He was the Son of God was by the miracles He performed. The key to many of those miracles was the faith people had in Jesus. What saved my marriage was the faith Jesus gave me!

It was only because of God's grace giving me the understanding and the patience for our marriage to get stronger. It wasn't easy, but regardless of the frustration I felt, I never gave up hope that Jesus could save our marriage. Deep down, I knew all that struggle and pain would end up making our marriage stronger. Prayer and a small amount of faith would lead to the circle of healing. I learned how God answers prayer in His time, not ours.

Romans 8:28: "And we know in all things God works for the good of those who love Him, who have been called according to His purpose." God wasn't saying Trinitie's death was right; He said that some good would come out of this tragedy. In everything that has happened in my life, some good came out of the bad things that happened. It took finding Jesus to help me see the good that came out of all my brokenness. God uses my experience to help others!

That morning we talked about Trinity with some joy in our hearts. I always called her the gentle giant. A lot of people would judge Trinity by the way she acted, especially members of her family. She never felt the love of being accepted; instead, people would judge her. The world is quick to judge others by how they look and act. If you took the time to know her, she was a special person with a kind soul.

Trinity suffered from Heroin addiction; Heroin buried the depression that was destroying her. When she was young, she lost Erick and shortly afterward started using drugs to numb the pain. Losing Erick, she suffered a significant loss. Drug addicts numb themselves, so they don't have to feel any pain. We went to alcoholics anonymous meetings for a short while, and we put her on methadone to help her withdraw from the Heroin.

Listening to Trinity share at the AA meetings gave me a better understanding of the pain and depression she was facing. One day she was getting down on herself; I asked her to go home and write down ten good things about herself when she would get depressed. Two days later, she had written down over 100 good things.

Trinity got a boyfriend, and they started going to the Church of Today, where she accepted Jesus as her Lord and Savior. My wife found her a better apartment, and she was preparing to move. By then, Trinity was off the methadone, and the therapist gave her Xanax to help with her anxiety. She overdosed because she took too much Xanax; my wife found her on her apartment floor.

My wife never talks about the day she found her; only her faith in God gave her the strength to clean up her apartment. It was only God and His power inside her that would keep my wife from ending her life. I can't imagine the pain she felt losing two children at such a young age.

We read about bad things in the paper and watching the tragic news that happens all too often, but nothing could be worse than burying a child who dies at such an early age. At Trinitie's funeral, so many people came up to me, telling me their stories of losing their children at such a young age. I would listen to their stories, and I could feel their pain as though it happened yesterday!

2 Corinthians 3:3: "You show that you are a letter from Christ, the result of our ministry, written not with ink but with the Spirit of the Living God, not on tablets of stone but on tablets of human hearts."

Paul talked to the Church of Corinth, comparing the old laws to the New Covenant God was making to them through Jesus Christ. God wants us to feel His Spirit not on tablets of stone (Ten Commandments) but inside our hearts. God wants us to feel His love and the understanding inside our souls.

Trinity taught me not to judge people. To take time to get to know people before we pass judgment. Trinity gave me a piece of her heart, and she taught me a lesson that will last a lifetime. Before I judge someone, I will take the time to know them!

Commitment

Psalms 32:1-2: "Blessed is he whose transgressions are forgiven, whose sins are covered. Blessed is the one whose sins the LORD does not count against him and in whose Spirit is no conceit." David wrote this Psalm; He knew God was the only source that could give him forgiveness.

When I am genuinely sorry for the sins, I committed God was willing to forgive my transgressions. The Holy Spirit is giving me the strength to make changes. I still make mistakes, but I am showing spiritual growth in all the weak areas. Slowly I was making more of a commitment.

For the person looking at this paper for the first time, you might say, "I can't commit entirely," this isn't as hard as it seems at first. God understands that we are human, and in many cases, this process will last a lifetime. But be grateful; you have a God who is patient with us. God wants to know we are trying to do the right things.

Psalms 61:8: "Then will I ever sing in praise of Your name and fulfill my vows day after day." David knew he had God's assurance by following his vows to God daily.

When I fulfill my vows every day, then I am committed to Him. Part of me praising God is by making vows and trying to practice them daily. We appreciate God's name by how we live and the love we show others. When pleasing God becomes a regular part of my Spirit, then I have the assurance that God will watch over me.

Psalms 62:8: "Trust in Him at all times, you people; pour out your hearts to Him, for God is our refuge." David knew the answer to the people was for them to trust in God. God wants us to pour out our hearts to Him. When I commit to God, I have security; knowing His ways lead to eternal freedom. Continuing to follow His path, I feel His comfort (refuge.) When I know God is in control of my life, His patience, hope, and compassion are always inside my Spirit.

Jeremiah was a prophet to the people of Judah (the southern kingdom.) God couldn't talk to the people, so He used prophets to speak to His people. He would speak to the people about their way of living and how it opposed God's will in many ways. Insurance, willingness, commitment were qualities that were a part of Jeremiah's Spirit. God used his talents to fill His purpose. Because Jeremiah had the assurance, we have the quarantee that God is speaking to those called to serve His purpose.

Jeremiah 2:2: "I remember the devotion of your youth, how as a bride you loved Me, and followed Me through the desert, through a land not sowed." Jeremiah was reminding Israel how God delivered them out of slavery and carried them through the desert. When I read this verse, I realize how much Jesus has done for me. I know staying committed is a big part of keeping my salvation.

Verses 4-5: "Hear the word of the LORD, O house of Jacob, all you clans of Israel. This is what the LORD says, 'What fault did your fathers find in Me that they strayed so far from Me?' They followed worthless idols and became worthless themselves."

Without the faith and the discipline that only God could give them, they became complacent. The people of Israel lacked commitment. Without committing, we will go back to doing things our way. You can't hide this treasure God gave you. The only way to keep what He has given you is to give it away. Committing to read the Bible daily is telling God He is worth the time we spent with Him.

Jeremiah watched kings and prophets murdered, but he still would remain faithful to God and His purpose. He prophesied about how the Babylonians would take over Jerusalem. After surviving the fall of Jerusalem, he was sent to Egypt; while in exile, Jeremiah would still preach to Israel's people. Despite the trial and persecution, he would stay committed to God and God's purpose. There will be times when we struggle. Being committed to God will keep us focused.

When I go through some emotional pain, I ask myself, "What keeps my soul in bondage?" How can I reach the promised land that God has waiting for me? What is keeping God's grace from entering my place of rest? Situations happen that are painful; if we stay committed, God will give us the strength to persevere. Being saved, I pick up my cross and pray for acceptance.

After we commit to follow Jesus, He will create a new life inside us. Even when we try doing things the old way, we realize it won't bring us true happiness.

John 15:5: "I am the vine; you are the branches. If a man remains in Me and I in him, he will bear much fruit; apart from Me, you can do nothing." God is the vine, and we are the branches. The fruits of the Spirit (love, peace, patience kindness, goodness, and faithfulness.) If we want those fruits, then we remain faithful to God. We stay committed!

Verse 6: "If anyone does not remain in Me, he is like a branch that is thrown away and withers; such branches are picked up, thrown into a fire and burned." The keyword is "remains." For those who remain committed, He gives us a promise in verses: 7-8: If you reside in Me and My words remain in you, ask whatever you wish, and it will be given to you. This is my Father's glory, that you bear much fruit, showing yourselves to be My disciples." When we stay committed, God's glory will shine. The more we remain committed, the more fruits we will receive.

A true disciple is a follower of Jesus Christ and has the willingness to learn. I ask myself, do my actions make me a disciple of Jesus? Am I truly committed?

Am I Committed?

Reading the stories about Ruth, Esther, and Elijah shows me how their commitment to God would serve His purpose. These people would go to any length to serve God. When I read their stories, I ask myself, "Am I that committed?"

Ruth 1:16: "Ruth replied, 'Don't urge me to leave you or to turn back from you. Where you go, I will go, and where you stay, I will stay. Your people will be my people and your God my God." After her husband's death, she knew following Naomi (mother-in-law) was the right thing to do. God's living presence in her would lead her into following Naomi (God's plan.) Verse 17, she makes another commitment to Naomi and God: "Where you die, I will die, and there I will be buried. May the Lord deal with me, be it ever so severely, if anything but death separates you and me."

Doing what was right would lead to meeting Boaz, and Boaz ended up marrying her. Being committed to Naomi served God's purpose in Naomi's life and ended by giving Ruth many blessings. Ruth would end up being the grandmother of King David. Boaz and Ruth had a son. Obed is the father of Jesse, and Jesse was the father of David. David was one of Israel's greatest kings.

Samuel is Israel's last judge. Judges is a story about men and women who delivered the people from their oppressors. In today's world of thinking, they were heroes. These men were not perfect; included in this group were an assassin, a promiscuous man, and one who broke all rules about hospitality; these men were not perfect, but they were submissive to the will of God.

1 Samuel, Saul became King of Israel, but God rejects Saul because he was disobedient. Samuel anoints David, and David goes out and fights Goliath. Saul became jealous of David's popularity and tried to kill him. Eventually, Saul was defeated and died.

2 Samuel, David, became King of Judah and then king of Israel. With God guiding Him, he would conquer all the surrounding nations. David was one of God's committed kings. Before a battle, before doing anything, he would pray for God's guidance and counsel. David wrote many of the psalms in the Book of Psalms.

David sinned by sleeping with Bathsheba, committing murder, and sending her husband into a war that he knew would kill him. There was a national rebellion against David. Because of his lack of discipline with his children, they got involved in rape and murder. His life in later years wasn't pleasant. Even though he went to God pleading for forgiveness, sin can still have its consequences.

After David died Solomon, became king of Israel. Solomon (David's son) became Israel's wisest king. He built a new temple in Jerusalem; he was the richest and the wisest king of Israel. He had hundreds of wives and concubines, and his lifestyle would worship false gods and had a spiritual decline in latter years. Solomon would write most of the Book of Proverbs and Ecclesiastes. When he got older, he wrote about wealth and wisdom being meaningless, how the only thing that had any meaning was his relationship with God.

At one time(Kings 1 and 2) were meant to be one book. These books give us the details of the kings who reigned after David. In this period of kings, God appointed Elijah to be their prophet. Elijah was one of God's favorite prophets; he was genuinely committed to God. He had to confront these wicked kings. The only problem with Elijah he was isolated(loner). He had to confront Ahab. Ahab's queen(Jezebel) was the most ruthless, evil queen in history.

Elijah would always confront Jezebel, causing her so much gloom. She wanted him killed. Being a loner, Elijah had to face his fears alone. Elijah was afraid and ran for his life. Reading 1 Kings chapter 18, you get a bigger picture of why the king hated Elijah.

In Beersheba, Elijah would leave his servant, 1 Kings: 19:4: "While he went a day's journey into the desert. He came to a broom tree, sat down under it, and prayed that he might die, 'I have had enough, Lord,' he said. Take my life; I am no better than my ancestors." Then he fell asleep.

All at once, an angel touched him, and he woke up. The angel told him to wake up and eat. There was bread baked over hot coals and a jar of water. After laying down a second time, the angel came back. The angel told him to go to Mount Horeb. The place Moses received the Ten Commandments. God gave him the energy to walk 200 miles; it took him forty days and forty nights(fasting) before reaching his destination.

Walking alone had to be one of Elijah's darkest hours, but after hearing the gentle voice of God, one of Elijah's greatest moments. God reminded him there were still people in Judah that believed. Elijah was committed to God and would do anything for God. 1 Kings 21:17: "Then the word of the LORD came to Elijah the Tishbite." Receiving instructions on what God wanted him to do, Elijah would go back and meet Ahab, king of Samaria.

2 Kings 2:11: "As they were walking along and talking together, suddenly a chariot of fire and horses of fire appeared and separated the two of them, and Elijah went up to heaven in a whirlwind." Two people in scripture went to heaven without dying; Elijah was one and Enock the other(Genesis 5:21-24.)

Ezra, Nehemiah, and Esther were people who were committed to God. All of them Had qualities that God used. Study their lives: you realize how God used them to fulfill His purpose. Reading their stories, I ask myself, "Am I committed?" Do I do what is right in God's eyes? (Ruth) Would I walk the extra mile to serve God's purpose? (Elijah)

Ezra led a group of Jews from Persia; He was a humble man who committed his life to God(Book of Ezra.) When called by God, Nehemiah would leave his job in the Persian government and go back and help his people. God used his ability to organize the people, and they would rebuild the wall protecting Jerusalem. Would I stop doing what is essential in my life to serve God's purpose?

Esther was King Xeres queen; God would use her influence over the king to promote the Jewish nation. Esther used her power to help God's people(Jews.) When called, the Holy Spirit lives inside me; do I use God's ability to help others?

God couldn't accomplish anything without dedicated people. Despite the people's rebellion, they continued to serve God's purpose. Despite how bad they would get treated, they were genuinely committed.

I know people who have served God's purpose for many years. Without their dedication, many churches would fold. If people don't commit, more will fold.

I will never be as committed as many of the people I studied in the Old Testament, but they inspire me to stay committed. What matters to God is doing our part. We live in a different world, but God never asks us to do something unless we can do it!

Do we take the time to volunteer? When money is needed, do we give generously? When that voice inside me says I should call someone, do I contact them? Am I truly committed and willing to serve God? When called, do we answer God's calling?

CHAPTER 12

Condemnation

Romans 1:18-19: "The wrath of God is being revealed from heaven against all the Godliness and wickedness of men who suppress the truth by their wickedness since what may be known about God is plain to them because God has made it plain to them."

Even though Paul wrote this letter to the Roman Church centuries ago, it speaks about the truth still happening today. Paul is talking about God's judgment(condemnation) on the people who suppress God's truth because they are wicked. When we rebel against God's principles and commandments, we live a life opposed to His righteousness; for many of us, it will lead to heartache and pain!

God is angry about all the wickedness in the world today, but He still gives us a choice on how we live our lives. When we oppose the will of God, we end up punishing ourselves!

Like so many in the seventies, I was part of the generation that rebelled against God. Because of the drug and alcohol abuse, many of our morals became second nature. We opposed many of God's laws. We ended up hurting ourselves and many of the people who tried helping us. In reality, we ended up condemning ourselves. In some cases, people ended up dying!

Many stayed obedient to God and their church; they would end up having good productive lives. For the people who rebelled, God became non-existent, and many churchgoers would quit going to church.

Romans 1:24-25: "Therefore God gave them over in the sinful desires of their heart to sexual impurity for the degrading of their bodies with one another. They exchanged the truth of God for a lie, and worshiped and served created things rather than the Creator--Who is forever praised. Amen."

We exchanged the truth of God for a lie. The lie is money, wealth, and relationships are what give us happiness. Making those things our priority only lasts for the moment, and then we would want more. As our generation developed; the family suffered, our children started to get into trouble; pills became the answer to our depression. Depression would lead to drug and alcohol addiction; many marriages would end up in divorce.

The family is a vital part of society. God created a mom and dad for a reason; money isn't a reason to not spend time with your loved ones; many neglected children become broken. Greed wanting more than what we need causing many marriages to break up!

Living together became a substitute for marriage when somebody involved children; they became the victims. God can't undo the brokenness from our past, but our brokenness would bring us back to God. That is why many people are coming back into the church, and many of them are finding Jesus. Forgiveness is replacing their condemnation!

Exodus 34:6-7: "And He passed in front of Moses, proclaiming, 'The LORD, the LORD, the compassionate and gracious God, slow to anger, abounding in love and faithfulness, maintaining love to thousands, and forgiving wickedness, rebellion, and sin.' Yet He does not leave the guilty unpunished; He punishes the children and their children for the sin of the fathers to the third and fourth generation."

God is talking to Moses and giving him the Ten Commandments. When we break those rules, we condemn ourselves. Our behavior can affect the lives of our loved ones to the third and fourth generations. Can you imagine all the heartache people could have avoided by following the Ten Commandments? God made those rules to live by for a reason; the choices we make can destroy people's lives.

The abused will abuse others. How our parents brought us up would be the way we treat our family. God made rules for living so we could avoid pain and heartache! Child abuse and neglect are still a problem in our society. Until we as adults begin to change, our children will have questions. How we teach our children will have a lasting effect on what they think.

The entire New Testament talks about being filled with the Holy Spirit and how it changes our life. Jim Cymbala continually reminds people of the need to be filled with the Holy Spirit. Jim runs a Spirit-filled Church in one of New York's worst areas. He claims we don't need any more interpretations of the Bible; what we need is for the Holy Spirit to fill our churches. The Holy Spirit will tell you what is right and wrong. The Holy Spirit will lay conviction on your heart about what you need to change. Even though people try changing what is in the Bible, the truth never changes!

Jesus is different than anything I ever experienced with religion. Looking back, I was a depressed child; how could I understand what God was telling me? God never gave up on me, but my lifestyle indeed ended any hope He had to reach me.

Romans 2:3-4: "So when you, a mere man, pass judgment on them and yet do the same things, do you think you will escape God's judgment? Or do you show contempt for the riches of His goodness, tolerance, and patience, not realizing God's kindness leads you toward repentance?"

Even if I didn't go to church or want any part of God, I still can't escape punishment! The walls I had toward God are falling. I am learning just because I walked away from God, and the church doesn't free me from His judgment. I am learning God isn't a punishing God; those living rules are given to help us avoid judgment!

Finding Jesus showed me a way of life that could lead me to eternal freedom. Even as a Christian, I can feel disapproval and think it is coming from God. I have learned the meaning of guilt isn't a condemnation. If we have a forgiving God, then I had to learn to forgive myself. A regret is an emotion man created; the only solution to not feeling guilty lies in forgiveness. With God's help, you can change. Instead of feeling guilt, God is showing me what needs to change.

I am learning when I oppose God's principles, I grieve the Holy Spirit inside me, and I truly hurt myself. My conscience motivates me and helps me see what needs to change. Some days we always war against human nature and God's way of how we should live. Even when I fail, I never quit trying to be the person He knows I can be.

My rebellion against God and his principles brought me condemnation. Finding Jesus and following His ways would lead to eternal freedom. We wage war against the evil that can creep into our lives, but the Holy Spirit has given me a choice on what road to follow. Jesus didn't come down to condemn us. He came down to save us from ourselves. Jesus came down to show us a way to keep our souls free from all condemnation!

Churches preach about God's condemnation, but how much suffering and pain we suffer ourselves many times is forgotten. Nothing is more painful than a mother losing a child at such a young age, as a parent watching their sons and daughters going down the same road leading to destruction and not being able to help them, how we watch our children suffer from drug and alcohol abuse.

For many coming into our churches today, we know the feeling of pain and isolation. Many of us paid the price because of the decisions we made. These people need the love of Jesus in their lives. They don't need to hear about condemnation and how God will judge them; they know how their sins cost them so much pain!

I have studied the Bible for ten years, and I never feel condemnation. The Holy Spirit shows me how I think is hurting me; then gives me the power to change. If my God was a condemning God, I could never measure up to His standards.

Running

Psalms 31:6-8: "I hate those who cling to worthless idols; I trust in the LORD. I will be glad and rejoice in Your love, for You saw my affliction and knew the anguish of my soul. You have not handed me over to the enemy but have set my feet in a spacious spot."

David had to deal with his enemies, but he prayed to God after feeling so much anguish, and God showed him spacious places where he had the freedom to move. What are some of the worthless idols we follow? When we cling to worthless idols(wealth, possessions, success), we tend to forget our allegiance to God. When the world and success got more important than God, my life got out of balance-running caused me so much anguish that I had a heart attack. God put my life on hold for a moment and showed me the way to a spacious place.

I was in the hospital meditating on God and what He is trying to teach me. When we listen to what the Holy Spirit is trying to tell us, we always have a spacious place. I had been running and trying to accomplish so many things. The running caught up with me, and once again, my heart stopped working. God shows us boundaries, He even shows us a path to follow, but the world and achieving my goals got more critical. Helping people, trying to fix problems, trying to make everyone happy caused me problems. Was I using the strength God was giving me to fulfill His purpose?

I couldn't say no; situations I couldn't control became more important than my family and the friends God put in my life. Doing what we feel is essential can become more important than the peace and life Jesus has given us. I was running, not taking the time to smell the roses or watch the sunrise or the sunset. I got so busy I forgot how it felt to be a part of God's glory. The life I was leading was taking all my joy away.

God can create miracles in our life by showing us what we can change and how I need to let go. I was reading and writing every morning; doing those things gave me the faith to walk out the door, but it didn't give me the strength to follow the path that would lead to eternal freedom. Part of staying grounded is going to church and my Bible studies, but other things became essential.

God doesn't make us go through sickness to teach us lessons; this resulted from doing things my way and thinking it would eventually lead to success. What I am learning is taking time to stop and listen to God. When the doctor told me another heart attack wouldn't be as favorable, he told me to look at my life and make some changes.

1 Corinthians 7:23-24: "You were bought at a price; do not become slaves of men. Brothers, each man; as responsible to God, should remain in the situation God called him to."

Slavery was widespread in those times. Paul was telling the Christians they were slaves (bought at a price) before they met Jesus, but they don't have to be slaves to sin. Jesus bought us at a cost (by dying on the cross) because He is part of our life; we no longer have to be slaves of the world.

I was running around doing things I thought would lead to happiness. Like many, I got caught up in this illusion of what the world calls success. God wants us to be successful, but He also wants us to stay grounded. Instead of listening to the Holy Spirit inside me, I continued doing things that were pulling me away from God. Even with loved ones, I tried to control situations that I needed to place in God's hands.

Meeting Jesus gave me choices on how I should live my life. For the first time in a long time, I started to listen. When we are sick or hurting deeply, this is an excellent time to ask God for his help. God put me once again at the crossroads of my life and giving me choices. Stay the same or learn my lessons; let God help or continue playing His role!

Part of my therapy while in the hospital is walking around the halls. I came to the south side and saw a sunrise that almost brought me to my knees. I saw the morning, and my eyes started filling with tears. I have spent a short lifetime running; at this moment, I was thinking; I can't run any longer. I knew deep down; I had to make some decisions that would change my lifestyle. At this time, when I truly need God to help me, I knew I had to make some decisions that would change my life completely.

I had all these ideas. I thought I was helping others, but deep down, my loved ones were not ready to hear what I was saying. I was doing things to help people, but those things weren't helping me. In that time of need and desperation, I made some decisions and started letting go. Looking at the scripture in Corinthians, I realized I was a slave to a world I created!

Another realization came to mind; God doesn't want me to die this way. We run, run, run, and in a moment, a breathes time, our life can come to an end.

I have a God Who waits for me patiently. He lets me do things my way, but when I am ready, He is always there inside me, waiting for me to ask Him for His help. It took my heart failing for me to get to the point of asking God to help me.

2 Peter 2:19-20: "They promise them freedom, while they themselves are slaves of depravity--for a man is a slave to whatever has mastered him. If they have escaped the corruption of the world by knowing our Lord and Savior Jesus Christ and are again entangled in it and overcome, they are worst off at the end than they were in the beginning."

The danger is the "they" we read about in this scripture. The "they" are false notions that their ideas will lead to success. Even as Christians following their ways (world) can lead us away from God's purpose. The world becomes our master, and we lose our relationship with our Savior.

God's use for us will lead to joy, but when His balance gets out of control, it can confuse. Peter is addressing Christians and how they go back to doing things their way. Many quit believing in God; in many cases, they will be worst off than when they started!

There are times in our life when life as we know it stops. At times like this, I can stop and learn. I praise God for giving me this moment. I will quit taking this life for granted and make some of the decisions that I can change. I thank Jesus for this opportunity.

God wants everyone to see the sunrise and the sunset in their life. Take the time to make your life worthy of God's glory. There is more to people than us saying hello. If they are open, spend the time to listen to what they have to say. Call the people God places on your heart. Take the time to tell your loved ones how much you love them.

Regardless of the pain that you might be feeling, take time to thank God for the moments that life causes you to slow down, and yes, if necessary, take that time to learn your lessons!

CHAPTER 13

Conviction

The truth you feel about a belief; a firm knowledge that always stays in your heart. Do I believe God sees everything I do? Do I truly believe Jesus died on the cross to save me? My faith in God can answer some questions, but are these beliefs (conviction) part of my soul?

Numbers 14:9: "Only do not rebel against the LORD. And do not be afraid of the people of the land, because we will swallow them up. Their protection is gone, but the LORD is with us. Do not be afraid of them."

Aaron was a prophet and a high priest. In this verse, he tells the people not to rebel against God, and God will help them overcome their enemies if they don't. The problem with the Israelites it would be human nature for them to rebel; they never knew the meaning of conviction. This time, the people were afraid, so they would listen to what Aaron had to say. Aaron was a man who had conviction, a strong belief in his heart; he knew the power God would give His people.

When I read about Daniel in the Old Testament(Daniel 1:8), he had a conviction in his heart that he shouldn't eat the food King Nebuchadnezzar wanted him to eat. At the end of ten days, he looked healthier than the young people who ate the food the King had to give them. Listening to the people in my Bible study, they would speak with so much conviction. I wanted the same trust and confidence!

James 1:5-6: "If any of you lacks wisdom, he should ask God, who gives generously to all without finding fault, and it will be given to him. But when he asks, he must believe and not doubt, because he who doubts is like a wave at sea, blown and tossed by the wind." I started reading the Bible every morning, and I started to adopt some of Jesus' principles into my life, then my faith would get stronger. Doubt was part of my journey; seeking to do God's will in all my affairs would lead to a conviction. I learned that this would happen in God's time; I never realized everything God had in store for me.

Hebrews 11:1: "Now faith is being sure of what we hope for and certain of what we do not see." This scripture describes the meaning of faith that Jesus died, and even if I didn't see it, I believe it happened. I knew (conviction) that God created the universe. I still had doubts about heaven and what would happen to my soul after I died. Something happened, and God would answer my doubt about heaven's existence.

I called a friend of mine. I knew the moment he answered the phone, something was wrong. I could feel his voice cracking as he tried telling me that his daughter Marie had died. They went over to her apartment and found her body in a closet. She was stripped of her clothing and put into a closet. The police were after her boyfriend, and all the details were on the daily news. Marie was 32 years old!

Jim and I have known each other for many years. I remember going to work, thinking something had happened to my step-daughter. I told Jim if a call came in to page me. Shortly afterward, I received word to call my wife, Trinity (step-daughter), who had passed away. Maybe a year later, Jim and Cindy found their son in bed. He passed away during the night. Erich was 21 years old. The autopsy revealed his possible death was an aneurysm inside his brain.

Once again, they lost another child at such a young age. What could I say to Jim and Cindy that would stop the bleeding? They were good people who never went to church. I was crying when I spoke these words to him, "I think Marie is with God in heaven; I know she is in a better place than this world she was in." The moment I said this, any doubt that heaven existed became a conviction. Marie and Trinity both suffered from deep depression. Marie and Trinity(step-daughter), both girls, were by-polar. They made mistakes, but their mistakes cost them so much heartache and pain. I don't think God will use his judgment and make them suffer even more.

Emotionally Jim and I have been through a lot in our lives. No mom or dad should have to bury their children at such a young age. Because Jim saw me go through so much heartache and loss, he knew my words were coming from my heart.

Shortly after Marie's death, I wrote a book, "It Starts With Me." God used some of the convictions inside my heart and helped me put them on paper. God reveals His will to me at His time. He shows it to me when I am ready to receive it.

I deal with people in Alcoholics Anonymous, and now with fellow Christians, I often have said these words to them, "Don't quit before the miracle happens." There is a miracle inside everyone waiting to happen, don't quit while God is working on that miracle!

Talking to Jim, heaven became a conviction, a strong belief that is in my heart. This journey I am on takes a lifetime of learning. I'm so grateful I have a God who is patient and kind. Aaron and Daniel were men who had conviction; God wants to build the same character in us. When doubt creeps into our lives, God's Spirit is saying, "don't quit believing; the answer will come."

Day Of The Lord

Joel 1:15: "Alas for that day! For the day of the LORD is near; it will come like destruction from the Almighty." This scripture was spoken by

Joel(prophet) to the people of Judah years ago. Repent for the day of the LORD is coming. Joel was warning the people to get ready.

In these verses, Joel is warning the people they need to repent. Their food source was getting cut off, the seeds planted in the ground under the clods. Their warehouses in ruin; God would abandon them. Joel wanted the people to repent.

For centuries, people throughout the world have heard this message. His judgment on the churches, their leaders, and those who have rebelled against God is coming. Scripture tells us before these events will happen, certain things have to take place. One modern-day prophecy that came to pass is Israel would become a country. When we study the Old and New Testament, many of the predictions have already happened.

When you read Isaiah, many of the things prophesied have already come true. Isaiah chapters 40-66 talk about a Messiah who will save us. The Messiah was Jesus, and yes, for many, that prophecy is being fulfilled. The Bible is still considered one of the most read books in history. People don't think all those events happened; I say to them, "Prove to me they didn't!" Throughout modern history, we find traces of these things happening, much more than they didn't.

Matthew 24: 6-8: "You will hear of wars and rumors of wars, but see to it that you are not alarmed. Such things must happen, but the end is still to come. Nation will rise against nation, and kingdom against kingdom. There will be famines and earthquakes in various places. All these are the beginning of birth pains."

Jesus is talking to the people about the future. These are just birth pains of what will happen in the future. He goes on in verse 9, talking about persecution. Today, Isis is killing Christians. In some countries, there isn't religious freedom. Many Christians still hide in shelters where they can pray and worship. Look at the coronavirus and how it shut down the world in such a short time.

God wanted one world, different places, but all of us believe in one God. When I see statistics, I often am surprised at some of what I see.

Since 1914 over 100 million people killed fighting wars. Just in world war 1, there were 8,500,000 casualties alone! Throughout the world, 740,000 die because of crime-related incidents! You would have to be blind not to see what is happening around us. God's prophets predicted all of this happening centuries ago. Some might think this is the sign of the times; I am scared to guess what World War 111 would yield.

Matthew 25: 31-35: Jesus is telling us about the final judgment. God will sit on the heavenly throne and separate the sheep from the goats. He will put the sheep on the right. These are God's disciples who follow the path He lays out for them. The goats are the people who don't believe there is a God go on the left.

Verses 35-36: "For I was hungry, and you gave Me something to eat, I was thirsty, and you gave me something to drink, I was a stranger, and you invited Me in, I needed clothes, and you clothed Me. I was sick, and you looked after Me. I was in prison, and you came to visit Me."

When we help people, we are showing them God's love and compassion. Many times God can only work His miracles through us. I feel all Christians should ask themselves this question, "Am I ready to sit on God's right side?" Am I using the gifts God has given me to help others? Or am I on the left?

Matthew 25:41-43: "Then He will say to those on His left, 'Depart from Me, you who are cursed, into the eternal fire prepared for the devil and his angels. For I was hungry, and you gave Me nothing to eat, I was thirsty, and you gave Me nothing to drink, I was a stranger, and you didn't invite Me in. I needed clothes, and you didn't clothe Me, I was sick and in prison, and you didn't look after Me."

Verse 46: "Then they will go away to eternal punishment, but the righteous to eternal life." When we start giving to others what God has given us, we will follow the path that will lead to heaven and eternal life. Our actions should speak louder than the words we speak. What do our efforts tell people about our God?

Acts 2:20: "The sun will be turned to darkness and the moon to blood before the coming of the great and glorious Day of the Lord," Peter was warning the people that indeed this day would come and to be ready. Peter was giving all of us a commission to go out and preach the gospel. The purpose of a disciple is to go out and plant seeds that can grow. People can see God's glory through our actions. God doesn't send us out unarmed the Holy Spirit gives us the strength to accomplish God's goals.

Why do we keep bringing up the Day of the Lord? If we don't, all can be forgotten by the generations to come. God wants to give people the chance to repent. Paul wrote letters to the churches warning them. I know this is a stern message, but many churches don't preach this message because they don't want to hurt people's feelings. Many pastors are afraid to lose members, so they stay away from chapters in the Bible because they are controversial. When I hear these verses, I feel hope knowing that my soul will live forever.

The reality is many churches pick and choose how they believe. The Bible speaks the truth; it seems at times everything that has lasted the test of time is being rewritten and opposed. You can't change the fact! Even our governments are rewriting God's truth by the laws that they are passing. People can believe what they want to think, but being a Christian, I can't rewrite the reality that I read in the Bible. It seems, in biblical terms, the Democrats are on the left, and the Republicans are on the right. There isn't a left or right in God's truth!

2 Peter 3:3-4: "First of all you must understand in the last days scoffers will come, scoffing and following their evil desires. They will say, where is this coming He promised?' Ever since our fathers died, everything goes on as it has since the beginning of creation."

People keep asking the question, why should they believe? Many will never hear what God is telling them. A big part of God's message is to be ready. That means trying to be a person worthy of the love God has given us. Regardless of when He comes back, I always strive to be the person He wants me to be. I spend a couple of hours at church every Sunday, but when I walk out the door, "We still are the church!"

2 Timothy 3:1-5: "But mark this: There will be terrible times in the last days. People will be lovers of themselves, lovers of money, boastful, proud, abusive, disobedient to their parents, ungrateful, unholy, without love, unforgiving, slanderous, without self-control, brutal, not lovers of the good, treacheries, rash, conceited, lovers of pleasure, rather than lovers of God--having a form of Godliness but denying its power. Have nothing to do with them."

Peter is warning Timothy to stay away from these people; Peter gives us a description of how self-centered his world had gotten. Look around at our world; nothing has changed!

Worldwide 275 million are exposed to violence in the home. In the United States, over 500,000 elders are being abused annually. Worldwide 6.9 million go to bed hungry that amounts to 1 out of 9 people are striving. Look around you, how many more shootings or children killing children can happen before we admit to ourselves we have a severe problem?

Look at the effects divorce has on our children! Maybe people should recognize God had a better plan and not obeying God's truth and its impact. The family is the glue that holds our society together; when was the last time you have gathered as a family? I don't say these things to make you feel guilty, but I want to make people aware of how much we have lost.

We might never see the Day of the Lord. But if I died today, am I ready to see my Creator? If I die today, would I go on the right or the left?

CHAPTER 14

Deeper Hurts: Learning to Let Go

God is always there for us. When we are hurting, we can always go to Him, knowing there is comfort in His arms. Many come to God as a last resort. Many who gave up on God are coming back. The entire New Testament revolves around the death of Jesus and how God raised Him from the dead. Jesus paid the price so that we could be free. We can repent and receive God's forgiveness.

Many that come are having problems with their loved ones. Some are going through a divorce; some have lost loved ones in tragic accidents. We come from broken homes. We all come with wounded hearts and scars from the past. We all come with deeper hurts.

Exodus 34:5-7: "Then the Lord came down in the cloud and stood with him and proclaimed His name, the LORD. And He passed in front of Moses, proclaiming, 'The LORD, the LORD,' the compassionate and gracious God, slow to anger, abounding in love and faithfulness, maintaining love to thousands, and forgiving wickedness, rebellion and sin. Yet He does not leave the guilty unpunished; He punishes the children for the sins of the fathers to the third and fourth generation."

God came down with a loving, compassionate heart. We condemn ourselves by sinning, and many times it affects the lives of our loved ones.

I was a second-generation alcoholic, and my son was the third generation with alcohol and drug problems.

We watch the pattern of alcohol and drug abuse or disfunction. Many who their parents have abused end up treating their family in the same way. The practice of alcohol and drug addiction can carry on to generations to come. God can't undo how we acted and conducted our affairs in the past, but He can help us change. Some will never feel any approval from the people we harmed in the past, but following His path will lead to better results. Even children abused in their earlier years can find healing in Jesus' arms. We no longer are victims of the past, but by asking Jesus for His help, we become survivors!

My dad had a problem with alcohol. My dad worked hard to support our family. The only time we bonded was a vacation; we took a couple of weeks every year. My dad wasn't bad; like many parents, we do the best we can. My dad grew up in Italy, and he never got the love of his father. My dad never talked about his childhood, and the sad part I never asked. He had a first-grade education, and even as a young person, worked his entire lifetime.

The only memories I have of him(in my younger years) was going to the bar and watching him drink. He would go to a neighbor's house and make wine; then, we would come home and get yelled at by my mother. While in a blackout, he hit my mother. Shortly after that happened, he quit drinking. When I started drinking, I became the victim. It was easier to blame others(parents) than to deal with my problems. After getting sober, I realized I needed to grow up and take responsibility. After I quit drinking, God gave me a better understanding of my dad.

God gave me the chance to forgive him. He was older, and they had to put him in the hospital. I remember going up to see him; I could tell he wasn't going to live much longer. I went home, and I started crying, and I said to God, "I forgive him." I asked God to give me a sign that He would take care of him. In later years my dad never smiled, I went up a couple of days later to the hospital, and he smiled three times. I looked at him and told him, "I love you, and I forgive you." That was the first time I said I love you, and it came from the heart. Two days later, my dad passed away.

I hurt my mom and dad in many ways as I got older. After I started doing alcohol and drugs, fighting increased. After leaving home, my mom never talked to me for four years. My dad tried reaching out; I remember him always going with tears in his eyes. The choices I made at the time were the wrong choices. She had every right to do what she did. After I got sober, I remember when she broke down and told me she was in so much pain, she had to let go. In the last two years of her life, we finally quit fighting.

With forgiveness came an understanding; it took finding Jesus to see all these things differently. Even though I was depressed since the age of ten, it wasn't an excuse to blame my parents any longer. I was sixty years old when I started to see things in a different light. I began seeing things through Jesus' eyes.

My son has an alcohol and drug problem, but I know deep down his real problem is depression. I haven't talked to him in at least six months. After I found Jesus, he told me, "If you tell me my lifestyle is wrong, I will disown you." My son is gay and married his partner in California, where gay marriage was considered legal. Except for a short while, after he got sober, our entire relationship was based on lies. The same things I did, the same ways I acted years ago, came back to haunt me. I saw the same rebellion, the same denial, the same behavior I had years ago. I thought God was punishing me for the way I treated my parents!

He didn't want to hear about Jesus and how He could change. I couldn't cope with his insanity any longer, so I let go and put him in God's hands. I know the fighting and arguing wasn't helping us to get closer. After 23 years of trying to change him, it was time to let go. Just because I let go, I pray for him every day. If he calls, the door is always open. I have given my son the benefit of not judging him.

DO YOU KNOW THE TRUTH?

Because of how I treated loved ones in the past and what I am feeling, I better understand the deeper hurts. There isn't a day when I don't think about Christopher and what is happening in his life. I decided to let go, and God is helping me to let go with love. Letting go doesn't mean I am a terrible parent; it means it was time to let go!

There was a prayer we would recite at our AA(Alcoholics Anonymous) meetings: God grant me the serenity to accept the things I cannot change, the courage to change the things I can, and the wisdom to know the difference. Amen

I am going through another book I am writing and thinking about my son, the title of this chapter, "Deeper hurts: Learning to let go." Instead of hurting, this is God's way of telling me I am doing the right thing. After I started abusing alcohol and drugs, my mother quit talking to me for almost four years. She never saw how Jesus changed my life, but she never stopped praying. I feel because she kept praying for me that God answered her prayers. God answered her prayers by giving her the wisdom to let go. Even if God doesn't answer our prayers, He still hears us. Many prayers are answered at His time, not mine!

The only person we can change is ourselves. Jesus is teaching me acceptance. I quit trying to fix everyone. Jesus gave me the strength to stop being co-dependent. I started working on the things I could change. I started working on the quilt and remorse that kept me in bondage. Wisdom means knowing what you can change and knowing when to let go!

I wrote this chapter a year ago, and my son and I are talking. God is teaching me what to say. I pray I am planting seeds that will help him. For some, the thought of having a Heavenly Father brings back many negative feelings. We all have deeper hurts from our past; we all did things we regret! We might never get the love we lost, but Jesus will give us the courage, acceptance, and forgiveness that help us move forward. Many times, letting go is our only answer, and God brings it back when the right time comes.

I talked to someone at work about our government's changes and how the pandemic virus has affected so many. Now, mind you, I listen, I can't be discussing politics at work, so I got to a boiling point. I looked at him and said, "I have a stronger conviction that God exists; the government can't change what I feel inside my heart; this year has healed me and made me stronger in areas that were weak."

This year made me look at how I feel inside, exposed some of my weaknesses, and healed some of my deeper hurts. I ended up saying, "This year has pulled me closer to God." For me, everything that happens will work for the good; Jesus will make some good out of all that has happened! Regardless of the world around me, God is always in control.

Even when I hurt, I am learning. I am not a victim but, with God's help, a survivor. It isn't my job with loved ones to always fix them; many times, all I can do is lead by setting a good example.

Do you feel you are a victim?

The pandemic was a condition we all had to face. Did this make you stronger or weaker? Did you learn any lessons?

Do you feel the only person you hurt by your behavior was yourself? That you don't need to make amends?

Depression

Depression can affect us in many ways. Almost everyone has experienced depression at least a few times, but it can last a lifetime for some who are depressed. Some of us can still function while depressed, but others need medication, and they still have problems. The long-term effects of depression can pull us away from God; in many cases, depression affects many of our decisions.

Over 19 million people have had problems with depression in the United States alone. That figure doesn't include the number who can function while depressed and many children who don't even know they are sad. That figure doesn't account for people oppressed or people who have committed suicide. All of us can agree that this could be one of the significant problems in the world today.

Two million people abuse opioids; statistics tell us 90 people die daily in America because they overuse opioids. It seems the answer for many people is using opioids. At one time, the widespread use of valium was the third type of significant addiction in America.

People used drugs to deal with their lives. Many of those people were deeply depressed. I don't put down medication, but there still has to be a solution, a plan besides the medicines we take. Our founder in AA, Bill Wilson, used mescaline to treat depression; this drug has the same effects as LSD. Anyone can buy marijuana for recreational use. Marijuana helps them relax, but does it heal the problem?

I went to a Catholic school, attended Mass every day, but I never felt the love of God inside my heart. The reason lots of things didn't register was depression. I was on two basketball teams that won state championships, ran track in high school; I only lost one race, which was in the state finals, but I never felt the joy of victory. Many of us were proper, quiet, obedient children, but people never knew what was going on inside us. The Catholic Church expressed the importance of obedience, and God would punish us when we did the wrong things.

The hippie movement started in my senior year. Shortly after graduating: I started using drugs and alcohol. The drugs usually made me more depressed. With a therapist's advice, I went into a mental hospital. Years ago, the only treatment they had for depression was shock therapy and changing your medicines. We are labeled as manic depressives, by polar, and in many cases, Add(attention deficit disorder.) After leaving that hospital, I vowed never to speak to a therapist again.

I got a good job; alcohol became my drug of choice. I started to believe the lie. Money, possessions, finding the one you love, I thought these things would make me happy. If you read the first book I had published, you would understand why my marriage failed.

I got sober at the age of thirty. Even after thirty years of sobriety, I still found myself lonely and depressed. I was looking at failing again, and my third marriage ending in divorce. My thinking at this time, everyone else had a problem, if only my wife would change.

I never looked at myself and my depression. My depression kept me from learning lessons; I looked for love in all the wrong places. I didn't realize, "It Starts With Me." Finding Jesus, I started to live a life patterned around the way He lived. I could see myself through God's eyes. I learned happiness is the by-product of getting some of the things we want, but Jesus gave me joy. Joy stays in my heart, regardless of what is happening.

I know the meaning of fear and the isolation it caused me. I know the feeling of holding on to pain because of the quilt I created. I couldn't let go of my past; I thought for years, getting those people back would lead to happiness. I walked around in a fog for most of my adult life. For the drug addict or the alcoholic who is using, all we do with our feelings is bury them. Instead of learning our lessons, we plunge deeper and get even sicker!

What Jesus gives us is a way of life that works. Many who come to God are suffering. God gives us forgiveness and the ability to start over. In my introduction, I talk about the Gift. The Gift was meeting a group of people who eventually led me to their church, and in the process, I found Jesus Christ. God is always waiting, but we need to be ready and willing to hear what He has to say!

Romans 10:8-9: "But what does it say? The word is near you; it is in your mouth and in your heart, that is, the word of faith we are proclaiming: That if you confess with your mouth, 'Jesus is Lord,' and believe in your heart that God raised Him from the dead, you will be saved."

I don't think I chose God; He came into my life when I was ready to listen. Emotionally, I was sick and tired and didn't have any more answers. I was depressed and felt hopeless. God was waiting with open arms wanting to be a part of my life. At that moment, I made a decision that would change my life forever.

It was a gradual change, but I started doing some things that brought me to my knees and the foot of the cross. God was leading me. Regardless of my rebellion and doubts, I was still moving forward. I learned to talk about my misgivings with fellow Christians. I knew this process takes a lifetime to unfold; success meant staying on God's path.

I started reading the Bible and living a life patterned around Jesus' principles. I got involved in two Bible study groups. God put the right people in my life. While praying at our Bible study, the Holy Spirit filled my soul; that night, I knew my life would change completely. I felt God's strength(Spirit)inside me!

It all started by confessing with my mouth, "Jesus is Lord." There are days when I hurt. I pick up my cross, and Jesus is there to help me carry the load. I am learning to live one day at a time. I handle life's problems and disappointments one day at a time. I have never looked back and regretted the life God has given me. I no longer feel alone and isolated!

Romans 6:23: "For the wages of sin is death, but the gift of God is eternal life in Christ Jesus our Lord." Many of the people who had problems with addiction would die at an early age. The way I was living was killing me eternally a little every day. The misuse of drugs and alcohol is indeed a sin. I had three choices before I met Jesus: death, insanity, or recovery. I could sink deeper into the depression and the loss of another marriage. Insanity meant I could do the same things repeatedly and, by running, expect different results. Recovery from depression meant putting my faith in someone other than myself.

We all have ups and downs, but my downs draw me closer to God and His salvation. I'm learning to persevere when I am struggling. Perseverance develops character. Instead of depression pulling me into isolation, I let my friends know when I am hurting. When I get down, the Holy Spirit shows me what I need to do.

Jesus offers us a way to live our lives. A form of energy that can give you hope. Finding Jesus gave me the tools I needed to keep my life moving in the right direction. I'm not telling you to quit taking medications that can help you; we are not therapists. I'm telling you God has an answer to the depression. A way of life that will lead to eternal freedom. Regardless of how far you have fallen, Jesus has a plan that can help you.

Looking back, I know God was watching over me. Deep down, He knew I was doing the best I could. What kept me from getting deeply depressed and going back to drinking was helping other alcoholics. I chaired or was always doing something for AA. Helping others helped me take the focus off myself.

I don't regret my experience, and even though, at times, it wasn't right. I know about doing the wrong things, about looking for love in all the wrong places, even the pain of losing loved ones. Because I know all these things, I can write. God uses my experience to help many people along this journey, but in the process, the person I help the most is me. Without Jesus in my life, none of this could have happened!

Devil

Nothing can be more painful to a Christian than having doubts. Doubts can keep us from getting close to God. Many go to church once a week, and that ends the time they spend with God. Without a strong faith in God, we don't have a foundation for us to build on. Having a personal relationship with Jesus will keep you grounded; in most cases, your faith will get stronger.

Satan uses any doubts in our character to steer us away from God. He tells us, "You're not good enough." When some bad things happen, "There isn't a God." When praying and God doesn't seem to answer our prayers, "Has God given you an answer to your prayers?" Satan can use our depression, low self-esteem, lack of faith we are feeling to destroy anything God has accomplished.

He uses moments when we are weak and vulnerable to plant doubt about God's existence. It's only by trusting in Christ and then trying to please God that can pull us out of the darkness. If you are a new Christian, he will attach any weakness in your character!

Satan is the great deceiver. He relies on our weaknesses to survive. When in despair or times when we are confused, he will war against God. Many come to God with broken marriages. The devil's first thing is to attach those relationships before God has a chance to mend them.

Looking back at history, Luther was good and righteous. He was one of God's highest angels. The problem with Lucifer he wanted the same power and position that would make him equal to God. Lucifer would rebel against God. God cast him out of heaven; along with Lucifer came 33 percent of the other angels. Those fallen angels are called demons. The devil is the ultimate anti-Christ.

1 Peter 5:8-9: "Be self-controlled and alert. Your enemy, the devil, prowls around like a roaring lion looking for someone to devour. Resist him, standing firm in the faith, because you know that your brothers throughout the world are undergoing the same kind of suffering."

Lions attack animals that are weak and struggling; Satan attacks people when they are soft and working. That is why Christian friends and our Bible studies are so important. When I am out of balance, this is when I am vulnerable.

Being Christians, we all have times when we need to deal with the devil and his schemes. I acknowledge what Satan is trying to accomplish. The closer I stay to God and try avoiding temptation, the harder it is for the devil to tempt me.

I am so grateful we have a forgiving God. Because of our faith in Jesus, His Spirit is helping us to change. When we try doing things on our own, it will lead to failure. All of us, at one time or another, will be tested.

Jesus fought Satan while in the desert for forty days and nights. Jesus knows the meaning of being tempted. He had conviction in His heart and the strength from God, and He could resist Satan.

It will take time and patience to develop conviction. We strive to do His will; the Holy Spirit inside us will make us stronger. Even when we fail, the Holy Spirit inside us gives us the intention to keep trying. I no longer count the mistakes; I measure growth by how much I have improved.

Ephesians 6:10-12: "Finally, be strong in the Lord and His mighty power. Put on the full armor of God so that you can take your stand against the devil's schemes. For our struggle is not against flesh and blood, but against the rulers, against the authorities, against the powers of this dark world and the spiritual forces of evil in the heavenly realms."

We fight a battle every day against the dark forces that can creep into our lives. I armor myself by reading the Bible every morning and trying to live a life patterned around Jesus' principles. If I have problems through prayer and mediation, God can give me answers. It's only by God's grace and mercy that I am still on this path. The Holy Spirit helps me to see my weaknesses and how they affect my relationship with God.

James 1:13-15: "When tempted no one should say, 'God is tempting me.'" For God cannot be tempted by evil, nor does He tempt anyone; but each one is tempted when, by his own evil desire, he is dragged away and enticed. Then after desire has conceived, it gives birth to sin, and sin, when it is full blown gives birth to death."

Being human, at times, we will fail! When we struggle to do His will, ask ourselves, "Do you want to change?" Sometimes we need to ask God to give us the willingness to change. We can change how we think. When we dwell on those thoughts, we give them more power. I know what my desires are and how they cause me pain. There are times I can't resist because I don't want to; I don't allow those moments to destroy what God has accomplished. Satan wants us to dwell on those moments, instead go to God and ask for His forgiveness!

Regardless of how much faith I have in God, I still will be tempted. I pray that when this happens, God gives me the willingness that can lead to change. I ask Him to show me how these weaknesses are hurting me.

Even though I fail, God lets me know, His wisdom and understanding are gaining dominion against the darkness that can come into my life. We are on a journey that is preparing us to meet our Savior. Change is leading me to be worthy of spending eternity with Him.

God knows we will fail, but He also knows how much we have grown. Failure draws me closer to God, and I realize how much I need Him; without His Spirit inside me, I wouldn't have changed at all. I know I am here only because of God's grace and mercy.

Through experience, I have learned that the more time I spend following God's path has helped me become stronger and capable of handling temptations. God is teaching me I am human, and yes, at times fall short of the person He knows I am capable of achieving. The Holy Spirit shows me how much progress I have made!

Discipline

Hebrews 11:37-40: "They were stoned; they were sawed in two; they were put to death by the sword. They went about in sheepskins and goatskins, destitute, persecuted and mistreated--the world was not worthy of them. They wandered in deserts and mountains and caves and holes in the ground. These were all commended for their faith, yet none of them received what had been promised. God had planned something better for us so that only together with us, they be made perfect."

Chapter 11 in Hebrews talks about the people in the Old Testament who had faith in God. Can you imagine how much hope and discipline it took for them to be faithful to God? While on earth, many of them didn't receive the blessings God had for them. Because of their faith and Jesus coming down from heaven, their suffering was made perfect.

Hebrews 12:1: "Therefore, since we are surrounded by such a cloud of witnesses, let us throw off everything that hinders and the sin that so easily entangles, and let us run with perseverance the race marked out for us."

It takes some work and discipline to change into the person God intended for us. The cloud of witnesses are the people mentioned in Hebrews 11; they paved the way for our salvation. They faced many trials and temptations that we will never meet. Because they had a strong faith in God, they overcame their suffering. We can be encouraged by their faith in God, and God uses their pain for His purpose. These Hebrews lived in a time when Christians were being hunted and persecuted, but God gave them the ability to persevere.

I still pray for the willingness and desire to change. Being human can cause me to stumble, but I ask God for His forgiveness and the discipline to keep moving forward. When life gets hard and God doesn't answer our prayers, many quit believing in God. Without the Holy Spirit in us, many of us coming to Jesus will fail. Jesus doesn't discipline us when we do wrong; He wants us to develop a stronger character.

Many of us never knew how to be disciplined, and we did everything we wanted to do. Jesus helped me understand the consequences of doing what I wanted to do and the negative results that happened. I was disciplined when it came to work, I spent hours perfecting my golf game, but this would only lead to getting what I wanted. God wants us to use discipline to get the things we need. God knew the Holy Spirit would help us to become stronger in all the weak areas.

Hebrews 12:2-3: "Let us fix our eyes on Jesus, the Author and Perfecter of our faith, who for the joy set before Him endured the cross, scorning its shame, and sat down at the right hand of the throne of God. Consider Him who endured such opposition from sinful man, so that you will not grow weary and lose heart."

Jesus understands the pain we can go through. Jesus knew, by dying on the cross and rising three days later, that we could be filled with the Holy Spirit; if we seek and listen, His discipline can become a part of our soul.

Verse 7: "Endure hardship as discipline; God is treating you as sons. For what son is not disciplined by his father?" So we will grow; God can keep His Spirit from us. God will never give us more pain than we can handle. God loves us enough to let us hurt; God gives us a daily reprieve depending on the choices we make and how we live our lives.

All of us will face hardship; it's part of the world we live in, but Hardship in God's world leads to discipline. Discipline leads to Christ and His strength growing inside us. God's control leads to wisdom. Scripture often speaks about attitude, and we should all ask ourselves, "Do hardships develop character and discipline?" When I feel God isn't helping, do I take time to stop and meditate, asking God why?

Verse 10: "Our fathers disciplined us for a little while as they thought best; God disciplines us for our good, that we might share in His holiness." Discipline is a way of God training us so we can be better people. God knows what we are capable of achieving. He knows that our life has gotten out of balance; at times, He waits for us to ask Him for help.

Verse 11: "No discipline seems pleasant at the time, but painful. Later on, however, it produces a harvest of righteousness and peace for those who have been trained by it." Habits, what we accepted as the standard in our past, some of those things have to change. Living in the darkness became a thing in our history; God's Spirit wants to pull us toward His light. Instead of being the darkness, God wants us to be His light!

Change can be painful; God spent forty days and nights in the desert while Satan would tempt Him. Despite Satan's deceit, God's conviction kept Him moving forward. We can achieve the same confidence by learning to stay in the light.

Verses 12-13: "Therefore, strengthen your feeble arms and weak knees. Make level paths for your feet, so that the lame may not be disabled, but rather healed."

When I meet my Creator, will I face Him knowing I did the best I could? Did I forgive the people that tried to hurt me? Did my thought process change? Did I intercede for people by praying for the people who needed God's Help? Did my actions help people that were disabled and needed your help? As disciples, does our example help the lame to see how Jesus can help them?

Verse 14: "Make every effort to live in peace with all men and to be holy; without holiness, no one will see the Lord." When we sin, we break the bond between God and ourselves. Doing things the old way could lead to losing all the discipline that I have gained.

Hebrews 12:15-17: "See to it no one misses the grace of God and that no bitter root grows up to cause trouble and defile many. See that no one is sexual immoral, or is Godless like Esau, who for a single meal, sold his inheritance rights as the oldest son. Afterward, as you know, when he wanted to inherit his blessing, he was rejected. He could bring about no change of mind, though he sought the blessing with tears(Genesis 25:29-34.)"

Esau had a compulsive personality; his impatience caused him many problems. Doing things without thinking caused him so much pain. Esau gave up his birthrights for a meal. He spent many years feeling rejected and seeking revenge. God still had a forgiving heart, and he would prosper. Esau had the same personality many people have today. We want what we want, and we want it now. Instead of being disciplined, we are compulsive. Many go to any lengths to get the things they want. They might get the things they want but lose themselves(their souls) entirely.

Because we discipline ourselves, we become more reliable. We can't get to heaven by working harder and making the same mistakes over and over. God's discipline builds character, and character leads to making better decisions. When we allow God's training to be a part of our lives, the journey becomes so much easier!

CHAPTER 15

Encouragement

We all know what it feels like when we aren't encouraged. We went through a significant change in our church. Even though I didn't want the move, the Holy Spirit gave me an understanding of how this change was good for the church.

A lot changed in the church; some members would leave, but God's Spirit stayed. God helps me see the good things that are happening. A kind (encouraging) word goes a long way when we build new friendships that God puts in leadership roles. Instead of criticizing the moves the new Pastor was making, I would encourage him. Being encouraging would change my attitude, and I could see the good Jesus was creating.

In the workplace, even in our homes, more is expected of us. Many times, we don't hear about the good things we do. So every opportunity we have to encourage people, this is a gift we can give them.

As wives and husbands, we should encourage each other. Instead of picking at each other's faults, please help them. Taking one for granted in a marriage leads to one not being validated. Not listening to them make them feel their opinions aren't worthwhile. Always having the last word makes us sound critical. Children that are not encouraged lose all their potential to grow.

Such is the case when new people walk through our doors at church. If no one takes the time to support them, they walk away from our church. God wants us to set aside any judgment or prejudice and to help them.

Philippians 1:12-14: "Know I want you to know, brothers, that was has happened to me has really served to advance the gospel. As a result, it has come clear throughout the whole palace guard and to everyone else that I am in chains for Christ. Because of my chains, most of my brothers in the Lord have been encouraged to speak the word of God more courageously and fearlessly." Paul knew part of his purpose was to suffer because he believed in Jesus Christ. We still gain strength and feel encouraged by the way Paul handles himself while in prison. His experience helps us to act more courageously.

Our actions, our acceptance, the courage we show others are part of how God works through us to encourage others. What we say can influence others. The same nerve that God gave Paul is the same courage God has placed in us. Part of our purpose is to share that experience with others. People can learn from our actions; how we handle sickness and adversity. Not being judgmental makes people stop gossip. While the church went through changes, talk could prevent those changes from happening.

Philippians 4:11-13: "I am not saying this because I am in need, for I have learned to be content whatever the circumstances. I know what it means to be in need, and I know what it means to have plenty. I have learned the meaning of being content in any situation, whether well fed or hungry, whether living in plenty or want. I can do anything through Him who gives me strength."

Paul was giving us the meaning of contentment. Being content in any situation. The keywords "I have learned to be content." Paul knew by dwelling on the negative things that he was going through would only destroy God's purpose. Paul could have crumbled, been angry; he learned to be content regardless of any situation. Even though it seemed Paul had the answers, he still would remain humble. He knew all his strength came from God. Paul would write 30 percent of the New Testament while in prison. His power while persecuted encourages us when we are struggling.

God has truly blessed me while on my journey. He has put people in my life that have encouraged and strengthened my faith in Him. Even while I was getting sober, God still put people in my life who kept me moving forward.

My friend Phil stayed in my home; he was having problems in his marriage. While there, he developed lung cancer. The first time God healed him, but three months later, cancer came back. Phil, throughout his treatment, would talk about having faith in God. Even the night before his second surgery, I remember how he expressed his hope. While in operation the next day, Phil passed away. It's people like this who planted seeds, to this very day, still touch my heart. I will never forget how he handled cancer and encouraged me in the process.

Philippians 2:1-2: "If you have any encouragement from being united with Christ. If any comfort from His love, if any fellowship with the Spirit, if any tenderness and compassion, then make my joy complete, by being like-minded, having the same love, being one in Spirit and purpose."

Paul wants us to share God's love and encouragement whenever we can. Paul sets an example for all of us to follow. Just like God's Spirit in Paul touched us, God wants us to share His Spirit with people we meet.

Philippians 2:3-4: "Do nothing out of selfish ambition or vain conceit, but in humility, consider others better than yourselves. Each of you should look not only to your interests but also to the interests of others." God doesn't make things hard. He wants to make this a way of life that can help others; when we are hurting, sharing that Spirit with others can make us feel healthier. I try being humble. I try taking the time to know people. And yes, when an opportunity presents itself, I try to encourage them!

We live in a constantly changing world; more pressure is placed on our path, even as Christians and the way we treat our families often takes on more significant challenges. Any time we take to encourage others is a gift we can give them!

Look For The Good In People

One of the worst feelings you can feel is watching your world falling apart, and there is nothing you can do to stop it from happening. I have felt that feeling many times while growing up. So, when I see others who are struggling, I reach out and try to help them.

My wife and I liked to dance. We decided to join a group and try to line dance. What we found was a dance group that taught us the meaning of friendship. This group didn't judge us. From the moment I met them, I could feel their warmth. They saw what was right and brought out the good inside us. They looked beyond our shortcomings and our weaknesses.

My wife had a daughter, who passed away, and her grief was tearing us apart. We had been to therapy, but therapy wasn't working. We truly needed someone or something to intercede. I think my wife was at the point of having a mental breakdown.

Many of the people in the dance group were Christians. After we danced for an hour, we would say grace and have a snack. They passed a prayer list around. They had a group who prayed afterward and included that list in their prayers. They loved us unconditionally. Many who attended those dance classes ended up going to their church and finding Jesus!

I remember one night someone was sick and going into treatment the next day. I was asked to go downstairs, and we were going to pray for healing. My thought while we were praying, what a great use of prayer. We formed a circle and laid our hands on her shoulders. For the first time, I began to understand the power of prayer.

DO YOU KNOW THE TRUTH?

The friends I met in that dance group are still my friends. We always do things together. My wife and I are members of that church, and I think the dance group has brought in at least six couples, and they too became members. We have different events at church. God is using that dance group and planting seeds.

Since making Jesus, my Lord and Savior, Jesus has put so much love inside me. I try sharing that love with everyone I meet. Jesus has given me the ability and compassion to help and encourage others.

I know how disfunction can destroy your life, but God uses my experience to help others. Jesus is in the business of mending relationships. He didn't come down to judge us but to be our Savior and lead our souls to eternal freedom. I never forget how God delivered me, so I can feel the hurt people are going through. I try showing everyone I meet the same comfort and understanding that God continues to give me.

People come into our churches; some have been in two marriages, many have problems at home and broken, some are gay, but God puts them there for a reason. Because some people judge them, they have walked away; they want nothing to do with God. It's not our place to judge them; we show them the love of Jesus and let the Holy Spirit be their judge. We never know how the Holy Spirit can change their lives completely!

I seek to do God's will in all my affairs; I know the truth, and the truth is what sets me free. The Holy Spirit helped me to see people in a different light. When people started to read my book, they begin to see me in a different light. I developed some relationships with other people. It isn't me that draws people to Jesus; it's God working through me. All we do is plant the seeds and pray. When we judge and criticize, we close our eyes to God and His purpose.

The religious leaders would ask God, what are His greatest commandments, "Jesus replied: 'Love the Lord your God with all your heart and all your soul and with all your mind.' This is the first and greatest commandment. And the second is like it: 'Love your neighbor as yourself.' All the law and the Prophets hang on to these two commandments(Matthew 22: 37-40.)"

The Pharisees in the church were scared that they would lose their position and power in their church. They never felt the love; God was telling them they needed. Even people we talk to are afraid of what they might give up. They don't realize Jesus can give them so much more.

My purpose is to share my testimony with others hoping it can tear down some walls about Jesus. I never know the overall results of how I touch others. God does, and that is what matters. It's a gift and an honor to be called a Child of God. I want to share the love He placed in my heart with everyone I meet.

Looking for the good in people, I learn so much about them and learn a lot about myself. Many times all I do is listen to their story. The greatest gift we can give is letting people know they are essential; we let them know that by listening to them.

The people in our dance group saw the good in us. I learned how God could touch our lives; by the way they treated us. I try to show everyone I meet the same love they showed me!

CHAPTER 16

Disagreements

With God's help, He will give us the ability to help people. Most of the time, when dealing with non-believers, all we can do is listen and plant seeds. We don't want to criticize and sound judgmental. If we are not careful, much of our testimony will end up in disagreements. Even our family might disagree with us. We will have differences; the Holy Spirit shows us how we can avoid our disputes.

On the Sabbath day, Jesus was going into the temple, and He saw a man whose right hand was all shriveled. The Pharisees were watching to see if Jesus would heal on the Sabbath. Luke 6:8-9: "But Jesus knew what they were thinking and said to the man with the shriveled hand, 'Get up and stand in front of everyone.' So he got up and stood there. Then He looked at the Pharisees, "He said to them, 'I ask you, which is lawful on the Sabbath: to do good or to do evil, to save life or to destroy it?'"

Looking back in Exodus, Moses told the people not to work or cook on the Sabbath. When it came to the law, Jesus broke the law. But in God's eyes, Jesus did the right thing. Jesus replaced the law, but we still need to abide and follow the Old Testament requirements. In some cases, this can cause a discussion.

I do what is right in Jesus' eyes, and I do what my conscience says I should do. If I help someone on the Sabbath, am I breaking God's rules? Was Jesus breaking God's laws by working on the Sabbath?

God made rules for our benefit; when I don't follow God's plan, I usually end up hurting myself. I try to follow God's laws, but the world has different opinions regarding working. At times those rules have to be broken.

We can analyze the Bible and question what it says, but being right or wrong, we can miss out on what God is teaching us. The entire time Jesus was around the Pharisees, they felt threatened. They missed out on the blessings Jesus could give them. We can get so caught up in our beliefs that we miss out on what Jesus wants us to hear. At times we need to take the cotton out of our ears and listen to what people say.

Even in the different religions around the world, their rules and how they believe are opposed to Jesus and what He is teaching them. How can so many people say they believe in the Bible, but their church and its policies contradict what the Bible says? Jesus teaches us to love, yet individual churches put up symbols, not wanting gays to walk into their church. How can we reach the non-believer by not liking them in our church? What does that say about God?

How many times does our need to be right cause non-believers to turn away from God? Before I became a Christian, if I saw Christians coming, I would try to avoid them. Non-believers have their rights. People would ask me if I was saved. If I said no, these people would say I can't go to heaven. These people never took the time to know me; who gave them the right to judge me?

I remember one man I would watch years ago; he was joyful and free. I would see him on breaks talking to a man we nicknamed animal. After he went to another department, I learned he was a Christian. To this day, I remember his actions and the example he set for us to follow.

In our Bible study, we have three who go to an Apostolic Church; along with them, there is a Pentecostal, a Lutheran, a Baptist, and at one time, a Jehovah witness. After the Jehovah's witness realized we would not change our minds, He ended up leaving. Following the advice of their pastor, the Baptist ended up going. If they stayed, they could have learned so much. Even when I ask a question, they always answered my questions by quoting scriptures.

We have disagreements, and at times have argued. From our experience, we stay away from what some of us believe. We don't always agree on some issues. I haven't had to compromise any principles. I don't choose what a person thinks, but the Holy Spirit inside me still decides how I feel.

Harley had been a Christian for over seventy years; he saw my frustration and would intercede when things would get out of control. All churches should have overseers watching us and guiding us in the right direction.

If I have doubts about what I believe, maybe what they are saying needs to be heard? I know several people, young and old, who are Apostolic, and I am genuinely amazed by how dedicated they are to the Lord! My brother-in-law was to become a Deacon in the Catholic church. He died the night before becoming a Deacon; he was the best Christian I have ever known. The point I am making I know good people in all the churches I have attended. No one has the best church or the only church!

Romans 14:1: "Accept him whose faith is weak, without passing judgment on disputable matters." We are mindful of new Christians; we don't pass our judgment on some of their beliefs unless we know that it will help them.

We will meet people with different beliefs; arguing with them wouldn't help either one of us. We can learn a lot because God has taught me to listen. Jesus has shown me that my actions can speak louder than my words. Sometimes they might ask for my opinion. The keywords," they ask." The best way to develop friendship is by listening to what they have to say. When we listen, the Holy Spirit teaches us the way we can help them.

Verse 5: "One man considers one day more sacred than another, another man considers every day alike. Each one should be fully convinced in his own mind." There are differences in churches, but what good does it do when we argue about right or wrong? Especially when both believe they are right.

The Catholic church believes the Pope has the ultimate authority to decide, while the Lutheran doesn't feel he shouldn't have all that power. The Apostolic thinks one should be submerged in water(Baptism), while the Lutheran church believes in water poured on a person's forehead. Would an argument help anyone get closer to God? The person who has humility will listen to what God is saying.

Some churches believe in the Trinity, while others don't. I need to know what I think is right. If I am doubtful about what I think, maybe God wants me to look at it differently? Maybe God is telling me to be submerged in water? The humble person will listen and try to understand. Sometimes even around our close friends, all we can do is plant seeds. When we argue, we are trying to change what they believe. What good does that accomplish?

Verse 10: "You, then, why do you judge your brother? Or why do you look down on your brother? For we will all sit before God's judgment seat." Some people look down on people; they think they are better because of their beliefs. Why do people look down on people that are weaker and pass judgment on them? Does it make you feel better about yourself? I didn't deserve the love Jesus gave me, but God welcomed me with open arms when I was ready. It's so essential for a person to feel welcome.

Verse 19: "Let us, therefore, make every effort to do what leads to mutual edification." Throughout the Bible, Jesus tells us what is right. In Romans chapter 14, He uses eating meat to prove His point. We can have different customs, and when we are around other people, allow them their rights to honor their customs. Many of the people Paul talked to were Jewish. So when in their presence, he wouldn't eat meat. As long as those traditions and businesses don't compromise our principles, we make every effort not to offend them.

Verse 22: "So whatever you believe in these things, keep between yourself and God. Blessed is the man who does not condemn himself by what he approves." God is nicely telling us that, at times, we need to be quiet. God is teaching me to think before I say something stupid. When a man condemns himself by what he approves, many will walk away.

Romans 15:1-2: "We who are strong ought to bear with the failings of the weak and not to please ourselves. Each of us should please our neighbor for his good, to build him up." Many Christians feel they are always right; they need the final say on everything spoken. We need to let people have the freedom to be themselves and not be critical of everything they do. Even in our marriages, keeping our mouths shut could cause fewer arguments.

Pointing the finger at them and telling them when they are wrong will only hurt them worst. Especially when dealing with our husband and wife, it will lead to more arguments. Sometimes we have to allow people the freedom to make their own mistakes. There is a right time to say what needs to be said; Jesus wants us to think before saying something that causes us more problems. Even before talking to certain people, I need to pray and ask God to help me.

If you have doubts about handling situations, don't condemn yourself and do the wrong thing. Learn to listen to your conscience; learn to hear what God's Spirit inside you is saying. When convicted to say nothing, then listen to The Holy Spirit(voice) inside you. We should try saying things that build people up, don't say something that will tear them down. We plant seeds that draw people to Jesus!

Philemon

God loves us so much, but do we deserve the love He gives? Do we reach out and help people God places in our path? When God gives us the ability to help someone, do we respond?

The most beautiful people I have met on my journey are the givers. They opened up their heart, many of those people were not productive, but whatever they had, they would give. Those givers loved me when I couldn't love myself.

The Book of Philemon is a story of how Paul helped a fellow Christian. Paul met Onesimus when He was in prison. Onesimus worked as a slave for Philemon; he ended up stealing from his owner and running away.

Sorry for the sin he committed; he sought forgiveness from his owner and wanted to go back. He wanted Paul to write a letter asking Philemon to take him back. Paul knew Philemon; he attended Bible studies at Philemon's home.

When we try doing the right thing in our lives, God puts people on our journey to help us. Paul had the power and the willingness to help him.

Acts 14:21-22: "They preached the good news in that city and won a large number of disciples. Then they returned to Lystra, Iconium, and Antioch, strengthening the disciples and encouraging them to remain true to the faith." Disciples are faithful followers of Christ; they live to serve God's purpose. Even in the King James Version of the Bible, the apostles are called disciples. God doesn't want Christians in word only; He wants people to be His right hand, His disciples. As disciples, we learn from God and spread His message to others.

Before leaving the city of Iconium and returning, Paul had been beaten and left for dead. A group from Antioch came into Iconium and turned the crowd against him. Paul's desire to be obedient to God was more important to him than facing the conflicts he had to encounter going back into these cities.

DO YOU KNOW THE TRUTH?

The Holy Spirit put passion and fire into Paul's spirit; instead of persecuting Christians, he became one of God's disciples; he would help Onesimus.

Philemon 1:4-5: "I always thank my God as I remember you in my prayers, because I hear about your faith in the Lord Jesus and your love for all the saints." Paul attended church in Philemon's home; at that time, Christians are persecuted. So for hundreds of years, they would meet in houses(house churches.)

Verse 7: "Your love has given me great joy and encouragement because you, brother, have refreshed the hearts of the saints." Before asking Philemon to do something, Paul knew how to address people.

Philemon 2: 8-9: "Therefore, although in Christ I could be bold and order you to do what you ought to do, yet I appeal to you based on love. I then as Paul--an older man and now also a prisoner of Jesus Christ--"

Paul could have ordered him as an apostle to take Onesimus back. Still, he wanted Philemon to do it willingly without having any grudges. He wanted Philemon to do the right thing on his own.

Verse 10: "I appeal for you for my son Onesimus, who became my son while I was in chains." Paul calls Onesimus his son because he became a Christian brother. Onesimus means useless; he was worthless as a slave and useless to God before becoming a Christian. Verse 15-16a: "Perhaps the reason he was separated from you for a little while was so you could have him back for good--no longer as a slave, but better than a slave, as a dear brother."

Verse 17: "So if you consider me a partner, welcome him as you would welcome me." Then he asks Philemon to let Onesimus back into his home. Being of good faith and willing to make amends for Onesimus, Paul tells Philemon, "If he has done you any wrong or owes you anything, charge it to me."

Paul would lead Philemon to Christ; he became a spiritual advisor to Philemon. Being a spiritual advisor is by helping people see the right things they need to do.

The book of Philemon is about a sinner's repentance. God used Paul to intervene and help his fellow Christian. Paul would approach Philemon by writing a letter without sounding judgmental or condescending. Philemon would forgive Onesimus and take him back.

God puts people on our path who need help. When the Holy Spirit puts it on our hearts to help someone, God will allow us to do the right thing. Making a phone call, spending time with someone, giving a small amount of money can go a long way in answering someone's prayer.

1 Thessalonians 5:9-11: "For God did not appoint us to suffer wrath but to receive salvation through our Lord Jesus Christ. He died for us so that, whether we are awake or asleep, we may live together with Him. Therefore encourage one another and build each other up, just as in fact you are doing."

People are coming across our path daily who need God's help. How Paul approached Philemon was with true humility. The Holy Spirit worked through Paul to achieve God's purpose. People cross our path who need help; The Holy Spirit convicts us to see how we can help them and gives us the ability to help.

How we approach people and try to help them truly makes a difference. I don't want to be the source of people walking away from God and not feeling hopeful. Being God's right hand, and with His guidance, I can help people by being the answer to their prayers!

Do you have barriers when it comes to helping people? What walls are in your home, church, or neighborhood? God uses Philemon as an example of how He wants to break down our barriers!

CHAPTER 17

Expectations

Deuteronomy !0:12-13: "And now, O Israel, what does the Lord your God ask of you, but to fear the Lord your God, to walk in all His ways, to love Him, to serve the Lord your God with all your heart and soul, and to observe the Lord's commands and decrees that I am giving you today for your own good." Once again, God reminds us that all He asks of us is for our good.

Jeremiah 33:3: "Call to me, and I will answer you and tell you great and unsearchable things you do not know." Jeremiah was a prophet God used to tell His people what He expected them to do.

On the verge of the Babylonians taking over Jerusalem and Judah, God was still giving them a choice, and "Call on Me" was a chance for them to repent and ask God for help. Eventually, Nebuchadnezzar and the Babylonians would overtake Judah.

God had a purpose in letting Judah fall; He knew this would draw the people back to Him. God knows if we will fall, but He always leaves the door open, If we are willing to repent and ask Him for help. When we rebel against what is good for us, how can God help us? The Old Testament is a reminder of how God's chosen people failed; reading these stories reminds me not to repeat history!

I remember coming home, and the house was empty. My first wife and son were gone. I remember getting on my knees and asking God to help me. What were my expectations that night? Was I expecting God to give me what I wanted? Since that night, I haven't had any alcohol or street drugs of any kind. I think to myself if my wife came back, would I be sober today?

After getting sober, I resented God. I would think to myself, why would he take my son and wife from me? I remember coming home after a long walk and sitting down on the grass. Overhead I saw thousands of birds going south for the winter, and the sky filled with sounds. At that moment, I could feel a peace I hadn't felt before. At that moment, my expectations of God began to change.

Even now, when my world seems out of balance, I can go to God, and He gives me peace beyond my understanding. Instead of fighting Him, I have a daily reprieve contingent on how I live. Even now, when I feel confused, I can go to God and meditate.

Matthew 11:28-30: "Come to Me, all you who are weary and burdened, and I will give you rest. Take my yoke upon you and learn from Me, for I am gentle and humble in heart, and you will find rest for your souls. My yoke is easy, and My burden is light."

When life crashes down on us, and we feel broken, Jesus wants to come down and be the yoke that binds us together. God is always there, reaching out to us with open arms. All we need to do is ask.

We come to God hurting, and He gives us compassion. I came to Him wanting, but He gave me what I needed! When we ask for what we need, God always will answer our prayers.

John 5:24-25: "I tell you the truth, whoever hears My word and believes Him who sent Me has eternal life and will not be condemned; he has crossed from death to life. I tell you the truth, a time is coming and has now come when the dead will hear the voice of the Son of God and those who hear will live."

2 Corinthians 5:17: "Therefore, if anyone is in Christ, he is a new creation; the old has gone, the new has come!

Jesus claims He is the Son of God. Jesus knows our heart; if we come to Him asking for His help, we will become new. Before meeting Jesus, many of us were dying, but we found eternal freedom because of Him.

After being filled with the Holy Spirit, my expectations began to change. I started gaining control over my emotions. I started learning the difference between my wants and what I needed. I started asking myself, "What does God expect from me?" When I am praying: how can God help me?

Jeremiah 33:6: "Nevertheless, I will bring health and healing to it; I will heal my people and will let them enjoy abundant peace and security." God always gave the Israelites a chance to repent and to call on Him for help. Because of the choices they made, they would often condemn themselves. The only way God could get them to come back was to abandon them.

God lays out a foundation, but we often do things our way, and we fail. Many times we have to fail before we are willing to listen. Many of us walked away from God, but He is always waiting and ready to forgive us. Jesus died on the cross, so we no longer are under the law but God's grace and mercy.

Ephesians 2:4-9: "But because of His great love for us, God, Who is rich in mercy, made us alive with Christ even when we were dead in transgressions--it is by grace you have been saved. And God raised us with Christ and seated us in the heavenly realms in Christ Jesus so that in the coming ages he might show the incomparable riches of His grace, expressed in His kindness to us in Christ Jesus. For it is by grace you have been saved, through faith--and this is not from yourselves, it is the gift of God--not by works so that no one can boast."

It's by God's grace that we are saved, not by our merits(works.) What does God expect of me after giving me this gift? He expects my gratitude and living a life worthy of His forgiveness. I spent a lifetime trying to get people's approval. Going to God was my last choice. I know by doing right in God's eyes, I will gain all the support I need. Even when I fail, I still am under God's grace and mercy!

God wants to give us more than some of the things we want. If He met all my expectations and given me what I wanted in the past, I wouldn't be the person I am today. Jesus has changed all my expectations, and I realize how He can answer all my prayers. I remember that night forty years ago and God giving me what I needed!

Eternal Life

Deuteronomy 30:17-18: "But if your heart turns away and you are not obedient, and if you are drawn away to bow down to other gods and worship them. I declare to you and your children you will certainly be destroyed. You will not live long in the land you are crossing the Jordon to enter and possess."

Moses is talking to the Israelites and all of God's children throughout the world. One of God's commands, not to put other gods before Him. If we follow His laws, we would be free. Think about how much suffering we could have avoided by following the Ten Commandments!

What do we feel is essential, and are those things more important than God? Is work and achieving your goals more important than spending time with God and your loved ones?

The way we live affects our life and the lives around us. There is so much dysfunction in the world today because people are breaking God's commands. Many live contrary to God's will, and many die because they don't hear and listen. Deuteronomy 30:19: "This day I call heaven and earth as my witnesses against you that I have set before you life and death, blessings and curses. Now choose life, so that you and your children may live."

Mark 5:3: "This man lived in the tombs, and no one can bind him anymore, not even with a chain." Verse 5-8: "Night and day among the tombs and in the hills, he would cry out and cut himself with stones. When he saw Jesus from a distance, he ran and fell on his knees in front of Him. He shouted at the top of his voice, 'What do you want of me, Jesus, Son of the most High God?' Swear to God that You won't hurt me! For Jesus had said to him, 'Come out of this man, you evil spirit!'"

Our eternal life is in restrain. We have isolated ourselves from anyone who can help us. All hope is lost. Jesus comes to us when we are in the depth of despair. Regardless of how far you have gone, Jesus can help you!

Romans 2:7: "To those who by persistence in doing good seek glory, honor, and immortality, He will give eternal life." Then in verse 8, God makes a righteous judgment: "But for those who are self-seeking and who reject the truth and follow evil, there will be wrath and anger." We all have a choice in the way we live our lives. Anger and wrath are terms God uses when we continue sinning. He uses harsh words so He can get our attention. God doesn't condemn us; we condemn ourselves!

We can struggle with our conscience and justify what we have done. Deep down, we know what is right and what is wrong. The only way to eternal freedom is to admit our wrongs. Reading the Bible, learning how God handles life shows us what is right and wrong. Following Jesus' example in our lives will lead to eternal freedom. Nowhere in the Bible does it say, "Do unto others before they do unto you." The Bible tells us to treat others the way we want to be treated. When others are mean, we learn to be kind and loving.

Psalms 95:3-7: "For the LORD is the great God, the great King above all gods. In His hands are the depths of the earth, and the mountain peaks belong to Him. The sea is His, for He made it, and His hands formed the dry land, let us bow down and worship, let us kneel before our Maker; for He is our God and we are the people of His pasture, the flock under His care. Today, if only you would hear His voice."

When I am hurting eternally, I can always go to Psalms in the Bible and read. When I read some of these verses, my Spirit can get in tone with God eternally. When we worship God, something good begins to happen; God becomes more significant than any problem we might be facing. When I feel weak, reading Psalms(Book of Psalms) draws me closer to God.

Psalms 39:4-5: "Show me, Oh LORD, my life's end and the number of my days; You have made my days a mere handbreadth; the span of my years is nothing before You. Each man's life is but a breath."

David is asking God for mercy; so many people want his throne. So, he continually goes to God and makes a plea for mercy. David knew he was a breath away from losing everything!

I feel God's love inside me. I see other people and how their lives begin to change. I know God is alive because of the strength He has given me. Having this gift God has given me comes with a challenge and a willingness to be a part of His purpose. It came with a desire to share this gift with others. I know for me to keep this gift, I need to give it away.

Shortly after being filled with the Holy Spirit, I was driving to work, and a voice inside me said, "Jim if you die today, are you ready to meet your Creator?" The voice inside me repeated the message two more times. For moments I was in shock. I called my friend. It took me a minute to talk, but he calmed me down, and I told him what just happened. He said; the Holy Spirit had given me a message. Two days later, another thing happened that showed me how quickly my life could end.

I was coming home from work. I was driving seventy miles an hour. The police were pulling someone over, and traffic was slowing down. I was slowing to a gradual stop. The car behind wasn't slowing down; at the last second, the front end of his vehicle raised, and he slid into the medium.

I never lost the memory of that day and what could have happened. Eternal life and committing to God took on a more substantial meaning. I knew this journey with God was real. I made a more significant commitment to God, and this journey I was on!

John 3:16: 'For God so loved the world that He gave His one and only Son, that whoever believes in Him shall not perish but have eternal life." We have heard this scripture quoted so often, but you can't understand the true meaning of eternal life until many of you ask Jesus to be your Lord and Savior.

There are people in the world today who are broken and need a redeeming figure in their lives—someone who can give them hope. God wants everyone to know Jesus and the belief that He can give them. "For God did not send His Son into the world to condemn the world, but to save the world through Him, (John 3:17.)"

John 5:24: "Very truly, I tell you whoever hears My word and believes Him who sent Me has eternal life and will not be judged but has crossed over from death to life." I was dying every day; following Jesus gave me internal freedom.

"In this world, you will have trouble. But take heart! I have overcome the world(John 16:33.)" Pain is a part of the world around us, but Jesus is more reliable than what is in the world. Jesus gives us peace beyond our understanding. The assurance knowing He is in control!

John 17:1-3: "Father, the time has come. Glorify your Son, that your Son may glorify You. You granted Him authority over all people that He might give eternal life to all those You have given Him. Now, this is eternal life; that they may know You, the only true God, and Jesus Christ, whom You have sent." Jesus is praying for himself and for all the people who have come to Him. You know Jesus if you feel your life has changed eternally. Eternally, you feel His Spirit inside you.

John 17: 6-7: "I have revealed You to those whom You gave Me out of the world. They were Yours: You gave them to Me, and they have obeyed your word. Now they know that everything You have given Me comes from You." Jesus is praying for the apostles and His disciples. If we obey Jesus' word, then we become a part of God's purpose. In verse 20, Jesus is praying for future believers; "My prayer is not for them alone. I also pray for those who will believe in Me through their message." Jesus is praying for us, being able to reach future believers.

Romans 8:9-10: "Those who are in the realm of the flesh cannot please God. You, however, are not in the realm of the flesh but are in the realm of the Spirit, if indeed the Spirit of God lives in you. If anyone does not have the Spirit of Christ, they do not belong to Christ. But Christ is in you; then, even though your body is subject to death because of sin, the Spirit gives life because of righteousness."

Paul is telling the Romans and future believers they have to be born again. By seeking to do God's will, they would be born again and filled with His Spirit. We learn how living in the flesh only hurts us in many ways. Learning how to please God would lead our souls to righteousness.

Many people are living a life that will lead to disappointment and heartache. God doesn't force us to come to Him. Having power over our flesh gives us the ability to grow eternally. When struggles come, we have a foundation. God wants us to have control over our flesh. God's Spirit inside us gives us choices. Doing things God's way gives us life forever!

Surviving Judgment

It doesn't matter; if we believe in God or if we don't. Regardless of how you feel, one day, we all will meet our Creator. How we live and how we choose to live our lives--here on earth determine if our souls live or die. If we want to be followers of Jesus, we should ask ourselves, would I survive judgment?

Mark 8:36: "What good is it for a man to gain the whole world, yet forfeit His soul?" Has the price of being successful been worth the things you have lost? Was searching for what you wanted worth the pain it would cost? Even Solomon in Ecclesiastes(Book of Ecclesiastes) tells us the only thing with meaning is God. He had everything the world could offer him, but toward the end of his life, it all seemed meaningless.

Has doing things your way cost you pain and loneliness? In Ruth's book, following God and letting Him run her life, she ended up getting everything she wanted and more. I found Jesus at the age of sixty, and he gave me all I wanted and so much more that I needed.

I see a world around us that seems like it is crumbling; the pandemic virus has changed the lives of millions around the globe. Maybe God is giving us a warning? Maybe Jesus is giving non--believers a chance to come and be a part of His salvation?

How we live our lives can cause our judgment. The way we treat others can render us God's judgment. How can Jesus help us avoid judgment? When the time comes, will I survive God's judgment?

Isaiah 1:2: "Hear, O heavens! Listen, O earth! For the Lord has spoken: "I reared children and brought them up, but they have rebelled against Me.'" Verse 4: Ah, sinful nation, a people loaded with guilt, a brood of evildoers, children given to corruption! They have forsaken the Lord; they have spurned the Holy One of Israel and turned their backs on Him."

Isaiah is prophesying to the people of Israel(God's chosen people). Under King Ahaz and King Manasseh, the people reverted to adultery, even child sacrifices to gods they created. God warned the people what would happen if they didn't obey His commandments. They brought condemnation(judgment) on themselves. Many in the world are still suffering discipline and review because of the way they live their lives.

Two things remain the same: 1. People can always come to God if they are willing to repent. 2. Sometimes, it takes judgment and discipline before we go and ask God for help.

Obadiah is one of the shortest books in the Bible. Obadiah was a prophet to the people of Judah, and Edom was a mountainous region around Judah. The purpose of this book--to show people God harms people who harm His people. Edom watched the Babylonians take over Judah. They had defiance when it came to God; they were cowards with colossal pride and took advantage of Judah's people when they were helpless. Because of the massive cliffs and mountains around them, they felt they were impregnable.

Just for a moment, think about America and what happened in 2020. Who could imagine this could happen to many of us. Then I look back at everything we have lost throughout the years. We live in a techno world but look at all the things we have lost. Have we gotten so blind to what is happening? It seems God is pulling His umbrella away from our nation. How can God help us when we constantly change the truth?

Obadiah predicted that God would destroy Edom. The Edomites were proud and thought they were invincible, but in the end, their nation disappeared. Any country that believes in its power, technology, wealth, and wisdom more than they believe in God will be brought low.

Obadiah 1:15: "The day of the Lord is near for all nations. As you have done, it will be done to you; your deeds will return upon your own head." Some people treat God's people with respect, while others don't, but one day we all will have to face God's judgment!

Matthew 3:7: "But when he saw many of the Pharisees and Sadducees coming to where he was baptizing, he said to them: 'You brood of vipers!' Who warned you to flee from the coming wrath." The Pharisees believed in their religious rules; they wanted others to live up to their standards, even though they couldn't. Sadducees relied on logic, placing little importance on faith. Both groups had one thing in common; they hated Jesus! Verse 8: "Produce fruit in keeping repentance." John the Baptist called people to do more than using words and following rituals; he told them to change their behavior(repentance.)

In verse ten, he gives them a warning: "The ax is already at the root of the trees, and every tree that does not produce good fruit will be cut down and thrown into the fire." He is telling people that Jesus is coming and He is more powerful; 11b: "He will baptize you with the Holy Spirit and fire."

Verse 12: "His winnowing fork is in His hand, and He will clear the thrashing floor, gathering His wheat into the barn and burning up the chaff with unquenchable fire." The inner layer (wheat) is the believers, and the outer chaff is the non-believers. Once again, in Matthew 13:36-43, Jesus tells us the parable about the weeds. The Son of Man will send out angels and weed out the kingdom. Everything that causes sin and all who do evil will be burned in the fiery furnace. At the end of the world, God will have His final judgment. He ends by saying the righteous will shine like the sun.

2 Peter 3:11-13: "Since everything will be destroyed in this way. What kind of people ought you to be?" We might never see the Day of the Lord, but we are still given the message of repentance and living a righteous life. Who knows when the time is coming when you meet your Creator!

1 Timothy 4:7-8: "Have nothing to do with godless myths and old wives' tales; rather, train yourself to be Godly. For physical training is of some value, but godliness has value for all things, holding promise for both the present life and the life to come." Paul is talking about spiritual training. When we work on godliness, we will grow spiritually.

2 Timothy 4: 1-2: "In the presence of God and of Jesus Christ, who will judge the living and the dead, and in view of His appearing and His kingdom, I give you this charge: Preach the word, be prepared in season and out of season; correct, rebuke, and encourage--with great patience and careful instruction." We need to spread the message about Jesus Christ and salvation. Verse 3-4, we are given a warning; "For the time will come when men will not put up with sound judgment. Instead, to suit their own desires, they will gather around them a great number of teachers to say what their itching ears want to hear. They will turn their ears away from the truth and set aside to myths."

What God says in the Bible is being replaced by people who feel things should be different. The truth is being twisted around so that people can feel justified(right.) The Bible is God's written word, but people oppose the truth. Society is bent on changing the truth(fact)! God told us the truth; when we fight the truth, we put judgment on ourselves. We make our choices, not God!

CHAPTER 18

Election and Justification

We did a study on the book of Romans. God opened the door and gave me a better understanding of why these words(Election, Justification) are so important.

Election: is an act of God whereby He chose those who would be saved in eternity past. "No one can come to Me unless the Father who sent Me draws him, and I will raise them up at the last day(John 6:44)." God, not man, has a more significant role in pulling us toward Jesus. With the urging of the Holy Spirit, we are drawn to Jesus. No one can believe in Jesus without God's help!

The question I often ask myself, why doesn't God call or elect everyone? "This is good, and pleases God our Savior, who wants all men to be saved and come to a knowledge of the truth(1 Timothy 2:3-4)." God wants everyone to come and be a part of Jesus' salvation. But many don't want anything to do with God. For others, God waits for the right time to draw people to Him.

Predestination: are we picked to be a certain way before we were born? God knows everything, but He gives all of us a choice on how we live our lives. Predestination is a false doctrine, a picture said to us by Satan. To think we are born to be a certain way is false!

Romans 9: 10-13: "Not only that, but Rebekah's children had one and same father, our father, Isaac. Yet before the twins were born or had done anything good or bad--so that God's purpose in election might stand: not by works but by Him who calls--she was told, 'The older will serve the younger.' Just as it is written: 'Jacob I loved, but Esau I hated.'"

I told you the story about Edom and Judah; Edom was Esau's descendants in surviving judgment. Esau gave his birthrights to Jacob. Edom wouldn't allow Judah any passage; there were constant struggles between the two nations. The nation of Judah descended from Jacob.

God has the power to know everything. He sees our soul and what will happen in the future. That doesn't mean God takes away the choices we make. God still gives us a free option on how we live our life. In the verses above, God is telling Rebekah about her sons' choices in the future. God uses the choices people make to serve His purpose. God knew what lay inside the heart of Judas and how he would betray Jesus. So God used his end to serve His purpose!

Once again, in verses 14-16, we are reminded of who God calls: "What then shall we say? Is God unjust? Not at all! For He says to Moses, 'I will have mercy on whom I have mercy, and I will have compassion on whom I have compassion.' It does not, therefore, depend on man's desire or effort, but on God's mercy."

God knows who will serve His purpose. God lets us wander for years in a wilderness we created. When we are ready, many of us are drawn to God. He wants everyone to come to Him, but only a few want to continue and seek to do His will in all their affairs. For the few who become disciples, God has called to be a part of Jesus' purpose(elected).

Verse17-18: "For the scripture says to Pharoah: 'I raised you for this very purpose, that I might display my power in you and that my name might be proclaimed, in all the earth.'" Once again, in verse 18: "Therefore God has mercy on whom He wants to have mercy, and He hardens whom He wants to harden." God always gives us the ability to choose the way we live our life. God knew how Pharoah would react. He knew toward the end; he wouldn't allow the Israelites to go freely! In the end, Pharoah made a decision that destroyed himself and his entire army!

Ephesians 1:11-12: "In Him we were also chosen, having been predestined according to the plan of Him who works out everything in conformity with the purpose of His will. So that we, who were the first to hope in Christ, might be for the praise of His glory." Just like these Ephesians decided to be a part of God's glory, we too, by determining (electing) to follow Jesus, become a part of God's purpose(called)!

Justification: God's act of claiming we are free from sin. God's righteous act of removing the quilt and the penalty of sin.

Genesis 12:1-2: "The LORD had said to Abram, 'Leave your country, your people and your father's household and go to the land I will show you.' I will make you into a great nation, and I will bless you; I will make your name great, and you will be a blessing." Abram(Abraham), who had faith in God, did what God wanted him to do. He was righteous and justified in the eyes of God.

Romans 4: 22-25: "This is why 'it was credited to him as righteousness.' The words credited to him are not written for him alone, but also for us, to whom God will credit righteousness--for us who believe in Him who raised Jesus our Lord from the dead. Jesus was delivered over to death for our sins and raised to life for our justification." The "him alone," mentioned in Romans, talks about Abraham. It also talks about us and how God needed justification(reason) to forgive us; Jesus died for humanity's sins. He became our sin offering!

Because we repent(genuinely sorry) and believe Jesus died on the cross for the sins we committed; God has the justification(reason) needed; to forgive our sins. Because we seek to do the will of God in all our affairs, He calls us righteous in His eyes. God knows that trying harder will lead to failure. Seeking is a conscious effort to know God. To set our minds on Him, and through revelation understand what He is saying.

John 15: 16-17: "You did not choose Me, but I chose you and appointed you to go and bear fruit--fruit that will last. Then the Father will give you whatever you ask in my name. This is my command: 'Love each other.'" God was talking to the apostles and His disciples(elected). Along with our purpose, God will produce fruit that will grow and the command, to love one another! Once again, "You did not choose me." Once again, God reminds us He chose us. The Holy Spirit shows me what I need; then I can go to God and ask!

2 Thessalonians 2:13: "But we ought to thank God for you, brothers loved by the Lord, because from the beginning God chose you to be saved through the sanctifying work of the Spirit and belief in the truth." God filled me with the Holy Spirit, I know the truth, and the fact has set me free. When I accepted Jesus as my Lord and Savior, I became a part of His redemption. Then the process of sanctification and glorification would begin. It wasn't me or my efforts that helped me change, but the Holy Spirit filled my soul.

Election: God had a purpose when we were elected to be a part of His goal. Many of us were sinners; we couldn't choose God so that God would choose us! He knew our experience could help others.

Justification: Faith is the element that makes us believers. We believe Jesus made restitution to God for the sins of humanity. We are genuinely sorry for the sins we committed in the past; God has justification to forgive us.

Redemption, Sanctification, and Glorification

God knew our human nature would lead to brokenness and how brokenness could draw people to Him. God had a purpose when He sent His only begotten Son down to earth. His plan would allow us to find redemption. **Redemption: the action of being saved from sin or evil. Saving is an act of correcting a past wrong.**

John 3:4-7: "How can a man be born when he is old? Nicodemus asked. Surely he cannot enter a second time into his mother's womb to be born. Jesus answered, 'I tell you the truth; no one can enter the kingdom of God unless he is born of water and Spirit.' Flesh gives birth to flesh, but the Spirit gives birth to Spirit. You should not be surprised at my saying, 'You must be born again.'"

Verse 8 continues by saying: "The wind blows wherever it pleases. You hear its sound, but you cannot tell where it comes from or where it is going. So it is with everyone born of the Spirit." We can't control what the Holy Spirit can do and how it fills our life. We couldn't contain our natural birth, so we can't stop our spiritual growth. Before this Spirit could come down, God would manifest Himself as Jesus, His only begotten Son.

Begotten; To be born. To generate is to give birth, to procreate, or to call into being. So God sent down, His only begotten Son. To understand the process involved, we need to study redemption, sanctification, and glorification.

We know from scripture that we were still under the law in the Old testament. You would have to offer up an animal as a sin offering to God in the Old Testament. God had to satisfy the law by giving us a perfect sacrifice, so He sent Jesus down to be a sin offering. A sin-offering among the Jews was a sacrifice, which provided atonement for sin.

Romans 3:22-24: "The righteousness from God through faith in Jesus Christ to all who believe. There is no difference, for all have sinned and fall short of the glory of God, and are justified freely by His grace through the redemption that came by Jesus Christ." Jesus paid the price for our redemption by shedding His blood(dying) on the cross! Because we repent(truly sorry) for the sins we committed, we can go to God and ask for His forgiveness.

Verse 25: "God presented Him(Jesus) as a sacrifice of atonement, through faith in His blood. He did this to demonstrate His justice because, in His forbearance, He had left the sins committed beforehand unpunished." Because we believe Jesus lived and died, and we are genuinely sorry that we have sinned, God leaves our sins beforehand, unpunished!

Matthew 27: 50-51: "And when Jesus had cried out again in a loud voice, He gave up His Spirit. At that moment, the curtain of the temple was torn in two from top to bottom. The earth shook and rocks split." The Holy Place, where only the Priests could enter, was split in two. Jesus died and removed the barrier between God and man. From the moment it happened, the law was replaced with God's grace and mercy.

The Old Testament law produced more sin; there were 700 laws plus all the rituals and sacrifices. God is all-knowing. He had to change things around so He could forgive people. Jesus overcame sin by rising from the dead. Following Jesus, we become a part of His redemption.

Sanctification: To sanctify someone, set that person apart from the person of the past. In the Greek translation, sanctification means holiness; To sanctify means "to make holy." Then comes the start(process) of making us worthy of being called His children. Romans 5:2: "Through whom we have gained access by faith into this grace in which we now stand. And we rejoice in the hope of the glory of God."

Verse 5: "And hope does not disappoint us, because God has poured out His Spirit, whom He has given us." By striving and seeking to be the person God wants us to be, we become a part(born) of the Holy Spirit. With His Spirit inside us, we become one with God. As Jesus promised the apostles, after He died, the counselor could come and fill our soul.

2 Timothy 2: 11-13: "Here is a trustworthy saying: If we died with Him, we would also live with Him; If we endure, we will also reign with Him. If we disown Him, He will disown us; If we are faithless, He will remain faithful, for He cannot disown Himself."

If we died with Him, our old self begins to change. The brokenness will start to heal. If we endure, keep striving, and seeking to do His will, we remain in His graces. At any time, we can disown God, and He will leave us. There will be times when we are faithless(hopeless), but God remains faithful because He lives in us!

Glorification: When our life on earth has ended, our soul's final stage and the mortal(human) body begins decaying. "But someone may ask, 'How are the dead raised? With what kind of body will they come?'(1 Cor 15:35.)"

Then, Jesus tells us about the resurrected body. Verse 42: "So will it be with the resurrection of the dead. The body that is sown is perishable, it is raised imperishable." God doesn't want our mortal body; God wants the eternal soul that is inside our body. In verse 43: Paul talks about our human body: "it is sown in dishonor, it is raised in glory; it is sown in weakness, it is raised in power; it is sown a natural body, it is raised a spiritual body." Our natural body is in the process of decay; our spiritual bodies will be new.

Verses 50-52: "I declare to you, brothers, that flesh and blood cannot inherit the Kingdom of God, nor does the perishable inherit the imperishable. Listen, I tell you a mystery: we will not all sleep, but we will all be changed--in a flash, in the twinkling of an eye, at the last trumpet. For the trumpet will sound, the dead will be raised imperishable, and we will be changed."

When Christ returns, in the twinkling of an eye, those, who have honored Jesus, God will transform their earthly bodies. You will have a spiritual body free from any sickness or disability you had to endure while here on earth.

Verses 54-57: "When the imperishable has been clothed with the imperishable and the mortal with immortality, then the saying that is written will come true: 'Death has been swallowed up in victory.' Where, O death, is your victory? Where, O death, is your sting. The sting of death is sin, and the power of sin is the law. But thanks be to God! He gives us the victory through our Lord Jesus Christ."

Christ's death overcame sin and the law; we will no longer have to fear death; our Spirit(eternal soul) can be resurrected and put in a new body(spiritual body.) For those who follow Jesus Christ: death will have no sting but victory!

Law and Grace

John 1:17-18: "For the law was given through Moses; grace and truth came through Jesus Christ. No one has ever seen God, but God the one and only, who is at the Father's side, has made Him known." God revealed Himself to Moses and gave him His laws and justice. Later on, God manifested Himself through Jesus, His only begotten son. Through Jesus, we received God's grace and mercy!

We never lose sight of the Ten Commandments and the laws given to Moses. After reading parts of the Old Testament, I begin to realize the origin of our fundamental truths. What I know about wisdom was written by Solomon(Book of Proverbs.) When I feel depressed or lonely, I can read the Psalms. We can learn from the mistakes people made in the past. The prophets give us an account of what God expects from us.

The only way God could control the Israelites was through the laws He gave to Moses. You were under law! In the New Testament, you serve a living God; we have a personal relationship with Jesus.

In the Old Testament, you had to earn forgiveness, but you are forgiven by accepting Jesus as your Lord and Savior in the New Testament! The Old Testament relied on human effort and obedience; in the New Testament, we are under God's grace and mercy. Does that mean we no longer are bound by the Old Testament and its laws? By no means, the Ten Commandments and God's commands still apply to the way we live our lives.

John 3:16-17: "For God so loved the world that He gave us His one and only Son, that whoever believes in Him shall not perish but have eternal life. For God did not send His Son into the world to condemn the world, but to save the world through Him."

Romans 8:3a: "For what the law was powerless to do that it was weakened by the sinful nature." The law, in many cases, didn't work because men had a sinful nature. Verse 3b: God did by sending His own Son in the likeness of a sinful man to be a sin-offering." In the Old Testament, sacrifices(animals) were offered to God as sin offerings. In the New Testament, God would send down His only begotten Son as a sin-offering. It continues in verses 3-4 by saying: "And so He(Jesus) condemned sin in sinful man, for the righteous requirements of the law might be fully met in us." Jesus met God's requirements(law) when He died on the cross. As prophesied by Jesus, after He died, the Holy Spirit would come down and fill our soul!

Romans 8:26: "In the same way, the Spirit helps us in our weakness. We do not know what we ought to pray for, but the Spirit himself intercedes for us with groans of words that words cannot express."

I wake up every morning. One of the first things I do is pray, then study scripture and meditate on God's word and His purpose. I have a personal relationship with Jesus. The Holy Spirit intercedes for me by showing me what I need.

If I fall short of doing things the right way; Do I lose God's grace? Do I get back into God's forgiveness by trying harder? God's grace is given to us freely; we can't earn it. We wouldn't be able to do His will unless we are under His grace. We have a daily reprieve contingent on what we do spiritually. We continue staying under His blessing by living a life centered around Jesus. When we do wrong, the Holy Spirit intercedes and helps us to do right.

God sees our hearts and how much we try to please Him. Many times people with a good heart can do more than the learned and wise. It's hard to teach the intellectual and knowledgeable; they have all the answers. God knows everything; He knows if we are doing the best we can. Even when I fall short of His glory, I am still under His grace. So I can go back and ask God for forgiveness.

You might say you are giving yourself the right to sin. I say we are human; we will never be perfect. I have a God that has forgiven me and loves me even when I fall short of His glory. It took me a small lifetime to find Jesus. Being human, we all will make mistakes; I am thankful we can go to God, and He is forgiving!

For the true believer, God's grace never leaves you. We all fall short of God's glory. Because He loves us, He is always willing to forgive. Struggling, working harder isn't going to stop us from sinning. Beating myself up for making mistakes is what the devil wants me to do. God(Holy Spirit) wants me to see how my behavior hurts me; He doesn't do that by punishing me. We do it to ourselves when we continue sinning!

Learning to stay in God's grace is a journey that lasts till the day we die. Having a personal relationship with Jesus takes our willingness and some discipline. Striving means were trying to do His will in all our affairs. Only God has the power to delete sin!

There is so much prejudice when it comes to God. I often ask people, what do you expect God to do? Some don't want anything from God, while others give me a list of wants. I seldom hear I want Him to give me what I need. I listen to people giving me excuses about why they don't want any part of God. They don't realize how much having Jesus in their lives can help them.

Matthew 20: 1-16; God gives us the parable about the workers paid equally. It doesn't matter to God how far we have fallen away from Him. Jesus is always waiting with open arms. I was sixty years old when I accepted Jesus as my Lord and Savior. He took a selfish man, and His grace has given me what I needed.

My Father-in-law lived a life opposed to God in many ways. After losing his wife, He accepted Jesus at a Baptist Church. I'm sure he had his reasons for getting saved, but God had mercy on his soul. He was in his eighties when he got saved.

Louis ended up meeting a woman at a Baptist church in Glennie, Michigan. This relationship was based on friendship. God had a purpose in putting them together. Louis gave up doing things he enjoyed and would help her. She ended up moving into his home; she stayed there until she broke her back and needed medical attention.

Louis, toward the end of his life, did the right thing. I believe in God and the miracles that happen when people let Him into their lives. I think God changed Louis and gave him what he needed.

Luke 17:15-16: "One of them, when he saw he was healed, came back, praising Jesus in a loud voice. He threw himself at Jesus' feet and thanked Him-and he was a Samaritan." The Samaritans lived in the Northern part of Israel, Samaria, as their capital. The Samaritans were a radically named society with Jewish and pagan ancestry. In this parable, God healed ten people, but only one came back and thanked Him. Verse 17-18: "Jesus asked, 'Were not all ten cleansed?' Where are the other nine? Was no one found to return and give praise to God except this foreigner? Then He said to him, 'Rise and go; your faith has made you well.'"

Only the faithful man(Samaritan) learned that his faith had made him well. I learned about grace because I remained faithful to Jesus. It matters to God if we thank Him; we praise Him by being reliable and committed. He can do so much for us, but we have to let Him in!

Galatians 3:26-29: "You are all sons of God through faith in Christ Jesus, for all of you were baptized into Christ have clothed yourselves with Christ. There is neither Jews nor Greek, slave nor free, male nor female; you are all one in Christ Jesus. If you belong to Christ, then you are Abraham's seed, and heirs according to the promise."

God made a promise to Abraham centuries ago. The same God Abraham served is the same God we do today. God's grace and mercy replaced the law that existed in Abraham's time. Because of our faith in Jesus and trying to serve His purpose, we become one with God's grace and mercy!

CHAPTER 19

Who Does God Want Us To Be?

Should we be shouting to the mountain tops, telling everyone about Jesus? Should we be quoting Bible verses to people that might save them? Even though there are a time and a place for doing all these things, I ask myself, "who does God want you to be?"

1 John 1:5-7: "This is the message we heard from Him and declared to you: God is light; in Him, there is no darkness at all. If we claim to have fellowship with Him yet walk in the darkness, we lie and do not live by the truth. But if we walk in the light, as He is in the light, we have fellowship with one another, and the blood of Jesus, His Son, purifies us from all sin."

With the Holy Spirit inside us, we, too, can walk in Jesus' light. Before I could shout about what God has done in my life, I needed to know how to walk in the light. Before God could purify me, I had to repent and ask Him for His forgiveness. I don't have to shout for people to hear or see me. I started changing, and people saw the change in me.

1 John 1:8-10: "If we claim to be without sin, we deceive ourselves, and the truth is not in us. If we confess our sins, He is faithful and will forgive our sins and purify us from all unrighteousness. If we claim we have not sinned, we make Him out to be a liar, and His word has no place in our heart."

The only way God can shed any truth on us is by our admission that we have sinned. When we admit those sins to God, then the Holy Spirit can help us change. The second part of repentance means changing the behavior that brought us to our knees. How can God's light be a part of us, but we live the life that brought us to our knees?

1 John 3:16-18: "This is how we know what love is; Jesus Christ laid down His life for us. And we ought to lay down our lives for our brothers and sisters. If anyone has material possessions and sees his brother in need but has no pity on him, how can the love of God be in Him? Dear children, let us not love with words or tongues, but with action and in truth."

We can't save the world, but when God puts people in our path who need our help, we should help them. Jesus showed us how much He loved us by dying on the cross, making restitution for the sins we committed. His actions spoke louder than any words He gave us. Our actions speak louder to people about how God can answer their prayers. God can work miracles through us. When called to be a part of His purpose, we need to hear His call. God wants us to be men and women whose actions speak louder than our words!

God is love. He wants us to be a comfort to people who are sick. We try to encourage people who need support—learning to listen at the beginning of building relationships. When I came to God, I was hurting. The people God put in my life treated me with love and respect. God expects me to address the people I meet in the same way!

1 John 3:4-6: "Everyone who sins breaks the law; sin is lawlessness. But you know that He appeared so that He might take our sins away. And in Him is no sin. No one who lives in Him keeps sinning. No one who continues to sin has either seen Him or known Him."

After being filled with the Holy Spirit, I felt the joy of God inside me. Non-believers judge our God by the way we present ourselves. People who claim to be Christians but live a life opposed to what God teaches only hurt Jesus and His purpose. God expects me to stop sinning!

DO YOU KNOW THE TRUTH?

1 John 4:7-8: "Dear friends, let us love one another, for love comes from God. Everyone who loves has been born of God and knows God. Whoever does not love does not know God, because God is love." God's love is in us, and we try sharing that love with others. We serve God's purpose by being loving and kind!

1 John 5:1-4: "Everyone who believes that Jesus is the Christ is born of God, and everyone who loves the Father loves His child as well. This is how we know that we love the children of God: by loving God and carrying out His commands. And His commands are not burdensome, for everyone born of God overcomes the world. This is the victory that overcomes the world, even our faith."

We don't pick God's family; we accept and love all His children. I believe Jesus came down to save the world. Because of Him, I am growing eternally. He shows me what to do, and I am capable of doing those things. He puts people in my path, and He knows I can help them. Sometimes all I can do is pray that they see the light, and then we can help them. Following some of His commands sometimes is hard, but we do them out of the love God has placed in our hearts.

The world plants messages about how busy we are or deny their presence and walk the other way. Haven't I done enough? God expects me to accept the challenges that He places in my path, facing those challenges that will lead my soul to victory.

1 John 5:13: "I write these things to you who believe in the name of the Son of God so that you may know that you have eternal life." He wants all of us to feel the eternal life that only Jesus can give. In all the verses above, God is light; God is loving; God is life. Because I love Him, I try to carry out His commands. I'm not perfect, but I know God is helping me grow in all these areas. I never quit trying to be the person God wants me to be. I keep striving to be the person who is worthy of the love He has given me!

Walking in the Light

Matthew 5:14-15: "You are the light of the world. A city that is set on a hill cannot be hidden. Neither do people light a lamp and put it under a bowl. Instead, they put it on a stand, and give light to everyone in the house. In the same way, let your light shine before others, that they may see your good deeds and glorify your Father in heaven."

If the Spirit of God is within you, Jesus is telling you that you are the light of the world. Don't take what He has given you and hide it. When you see someone who needs Jesus, don't walk the other way. When you have a chance to tell people about Jesus, don't be silent. Jesus has given you the Holy Spirit, but don't hide Him under a bowl. God has given you the ability to help others when you use what He has given you, lead people to believe, and glorify your Father in heaven!

Mark 4:24-25: "Consider carefully what you hear, He continued. With the measure you use, it will be measured to you--and even more, whatever does not have, even what they have will be taken from them."

When we help people, Jesus puts on our path He will give us more to do. But for those who call themselves Christians and do nothing, what you have eventually will be taken away. We are the light, but you have to give it away if we want to keep the light. That light will grow by sharing it with others.

Reading the Book of James gives us a guide on how to stay in the light. This book exposes practices that hurt God's word and tells us how to live in God's light. Each chapter gives us a summary of how we should live our lives. Chapter one: We must endure trials and temptation. Do what the word says we should do! Chapter two: Compassionate service. We treat people the same-Chapter three: Proper use of our tongue. Faith without works is dead. Chapter 4: Do I submit to God's word? Am I remorseful, repentant, sorry when I hurt others? Am I humble? Chapter 5: Patience when you are suffering and the prayer of faith.

James 1:2-4: "Consider it pure joy, my brothers, whenever you face trials of many kinds because you know that the testing of your faith develops perseverance. Perseverance must finish its work so that you may be mature and complete, not lacking anything."

A big part of getting stronger is by building character. Trials, growing pains, at times, we will be tested, but because we persevere, facing all this will make us stronger. We learn to ask God for help through trying times; pain draws us closer to God. We learn about the weaknesses in our character. If we want to stay in the light, we start dealing with ourselves and those weaknesses!

Verse 12: "Blessed is the man who perseveres under trial because when he has stood the test, he will receive the crown of life that God has promised to those who love him." The crown of life the athlete gets is a wreath saying He has won. The height of being a disciple is eternal life with God that will last an eternity.

Verse 13-15: "When tempted, no one should say, 'God is tempting me.' God cannot be tempted by evil, nor does He tempt anyone; but each one is tempted when, by his own evil desire, he is dragged away and enticed. Then, after desire is conceived, it gives birth to sin; and sin, when it is full-grown, gives birth to death." Looking back, did we use all our desires for their intended purpose?

The Holy Spirit showed me the excessive use of my desires caused me so much pain. Lust, gluttony, greed, even my pride, and striving to get ahead would lead to wanting more. The willingness to love would lead to moments of satisfaction(lust.) The excessive abuse of food(gluttony) would lead to sickness in later years. False pride keeps us from seeing the things God wants us to see. My way of doing things usually opposes the will of God. My ego becomes more important than the humility that pulls us closer to God.

Verses 22-24: "Do not merely listen to the word and so deceive yourselves. Do what it says, anyone who listens to the word but does not do what it says is like a man who looks at his face in the mirror and, after looking at himself, goes away and immediately forgets what he looks like."

I have to listen to what I am reading in the Bible and do what it says to do. What good is reading the Bible if I don't practice what it is teaching me? The balkers(unbelievers) always put down the way Jesus lived His life. I ask myself, what good is reading the Bible every day, but I continue living in a way that opposes His righteousness? Isn't that being a hypocrite!

James 2:1: "My brothers, as believers in our Lord Jesus Christ, don't show favoritism." Jesus wants us to treat everyone the same. Don't let your judgment cloud out His purpose.

Verse 14: "What good is it, my brothers, if a man claims to have faith but has no deeds?" God uses an example of a man who comes to you needing clothes. You sit and listen, you might say a prayer, but regardless of the fact you have plenty of money, you walk away. What does your faith tell that person about the God you serve? Verse 18: "But someone will say, 'You have faith; I have deeds.' Show me your faith without deeds, and I will show you my faith by what I do." Jesus wants doers of our word, not only by the words we speak but by our deeds!

James 3:9-12: "With the tongue, we praise our Lord and Father, and with it, we curse men, who have been made in God's likeness. Out of the same mouth come praise and cursing. My brothers, this should not be. Can both freshwater and saltwater flow from the same spring? My brothers, can a fig tree bear olives, or a grapevine grow figs? Neither can a salt spring produce fresh water?" There isn't a middle road in the light. You are either walking in the light or not in God's light. People know if we are truthful by our actions and what we say when we are talking.

James 3:13-14: "Who is wise and understanding among you? Let him show it by his good life, by deeds done in the humility that comes from wisdom. But if you harbor bitter envy and selfish ambition in your hearts, do not boast about it or deny the truth."

It goes on by saying such wisdom does not come down from heaven. Verse 16-18: "For where you have envy and selfish behavior, there you find disorder and every evil practice. But the wisdom that comes from heaven is first of all pure; peace-loving, considerate, submissive, full of mercy and good fruit, impartial and sincere. Peacemakers who sow in peace raise a harvest of righteousness."

Some people claim to be wise, but you see how foliage they are when you listen to them. Even the way you conduct your affairs keeps them from seeing the light of Jesus. When we harbor envy and selfish behavior in our hearts, we no longer are in the light.

"You adulteries people, don't you know friendship with the world is hatred toward God? Anyone who chooses to be a friend of the world becomes an enemy of God, (James 4:4.)" When the world and its ideas become more important than God's purpose, we can get lost, and we become enemies of what God is trying to say to us.

Verse 5-6 goes on by saying: "Or do you think Scripture says without reason that the Spirit He put in us envies intensely? But He gives us more grace. That is why Scripture says: 'God opposes the proud, but gives grace to the humble.'"

When you have wandered away from the light, humble yourself, and ask God to help you. When we are truly sorry, God is always willing to forgive us.

The prayer of faith: "Is anyone of you in trouble? He should pray. Is anyone happy? Let him sing songs of praise. Is anyone of you sick? He should call on the elders of the church to pray over him and anoint him with oil in the name of the Lord. And the prayer offered in faith will make him well; the Lord will raise him up. If he has sinned, he is forgiven. Therefore confess your sins to each other and pray for each other so that you may be healed. The prayer of a righteous man is powerful and effective."

Being a doer of God's word means I am obedient to His ways. Regardless of what I am going through, I am patient and keep my eyes on God and His salvation. When I am weak, I admit to those weaknesses and ask people to pray for me. Because I have shortcomings, God can show me how to do the opposite. God can give me a course of action that will help me.

John 1:4-5: "In Him was life, and the life was the light of men. And the light shineth in darkness; and the darkness has not understood it." Before meeting Jesus, I was living in the darkness, hoping for a miracle.

The miracle started when I asked Jesus to be my Lord and Savior. The second miracle that happened, following His ways, would lead me into seeing the light. The third miracle that happened; understanding the meaning of Jesus and His purpose living inside me, my faith in Jesus would grow stronger. The fourth miracle that happened, I was the light!

What the World Needs

We can go to church on Sunday, but what happens to us after we leave? My Pastors have always taught us we are the church; when we leave, people will judge God by what they see and feel. I ask myself, what is the quality that separates me from others? What qualities do I need that can draw people to God and His comfort? What degree of excellence do I base my life around? We know Jesus was forgiving, but what quality does He have that pulls us into Him?

1 Corinthians 13:1: "If I speak in the tongues of men and angels, but have not love, I am only a resounding gong or a clanging cymbal." What separates Jesus from everyone is the passion that He gives us freely. His love for humanity gave Him the strength to sacrifice His own life. He left His place of glory to become a servant to the ones below Him. To many, we are sounding boards. To many, all we can give them is our love!

Verse 2: "If I have the gift of prophecy and can fathom all mysteries and all knowledge, and if I have a faith that can move mountains, but have not love, I am nothing." We can get so caught up in this world; we seldom have the time or energy to share our time with others. People know, we know, we can quote verses that can challenge them. You seem to have faith that can move mountains, but the love and compassion inside me give my words meaning.

Verse 3: " If I give all I possess to the poor and surrender my body to the flames, but have not love, I gain nothing." God wants to feel our love; He wants the giver to be gracious in all he does. Giving because we have to offer, sacrifice beyond sacrifice means nothing to God unless we do these things out of love!

Verse 4: "Love is patient; love is kind. It does not envy; it does not boast; it is not proud." People know we have love because we are patient and kind. We don't brag about our accomplishments. It goes on to say that we are forgiving; that means we don't hold grudges. We don't delight because people are suffering.

Love is not being rude; do I sound condescending and critical? Do I allow others the ability to voice their opinions? Do you allow people the freedom to be themselves? Love rejoices in knowing God's truth. It perseveres when saying something wouldn't help anyone.

Verse 9-10: "For we know in part and we prophesy in part, but when perfection comes, the imperfect disappears." God gives all of us spiritual gifts. He wants us to use them to encourage and give people hope. We don't use these gifts for our gain; It isn't about getting ahead and the number of souls we can save. When our motives are pure and driven by the Holy Spirit, everyone should feel our love. When we think about ourselves, then we no longer are loving. In verse 11: Jesus wants us to put our childish behavior behind us!

The Corinth Church had gotten morally corrupt, and the real meaning of love was misused. We too can abuse the love God has given us. We live in a world that bases its happiness on getting the things we want. God's nature never changes; He is always willing and loving enough to give us what we need. Love is God's greatest weapon against the hatred that lives in the world around us. The scriptures continuously remind us to be kind to our enemies.

Jesus based his life around faith, hope, and love. Faith gives us a foundation. Hope gives us focus, but love binds everything together. Without love, it would mean nothing!

How Does God Measure Greatness

How do you measure greatness? Do you measure importance by how much money you have and what you own? Does my formula for greatness lead my soul to eternal freedom? Do my priorities lead to prominence in the eyes of God?

When we study the Book of Judges, we see how Israel reacted after being freed from slavery. They took God for granted. They never felt the joy of knowing God would give them everything they needed. They became slaves to all their passions.

In the Book of Judges, we read the story about Samson and Delilah. While in Gaza, Samson went to a prostitute(Deliah); the Philistines(Israel's enemy) heard he was in the city. So they went to Delilah, hoping she could seduce him and learn the secret of his high strength. Delilah valued money, so she ended up seducing Samson and learned how to break his power.

Samson, in a time of weakness, told her how to make him lose his power. While sleeping, she called a man in and had his seven braids of hair cut. We know Samson lost all his strength. The moral of the story was the misuse of power that God had given Samson. Because of his weaknesses(wants), he lost all his control!

Instead of using the gifts God gives us for His glory, some misuse those gifts for personal gain. Because they don't act wisely, they hurt themselves and others. We take natural desires and blow them out of proportion. We misuse the gifts God has given us and their intended purpose. In the process, we become slaves to those desires. Samson's desires destroyed his ability to help his people. Our desires and how we achieve greatness can keep us from serving God.

Matthew 20:26-28: "Not so with you. Instead, whoever wants to be great among you must be a servant, and whoever wants to be first must be your slave--just as the Son of God did not come to be served, but to serve, and to give His life as a ransom for many." Jesus talked to the people about service, His service to God, and how service is part of our purpose. Jesus came down from heaven to be a service to us. Never has Jesus intended use been to serve Himself. He came to help us!

Jesus doesn't ask us to do things that He wouldn't do. He set an example for all of us to follow. We become a part of His greatness and one with His Spirit by sharing our love and compassion with others. We become disciples by being His follower. We learn and listen. We are not doormats to society; we use the gifts and our ability wisely.

John the Baptist and all of Jesus' people were ordinary people. Jesus touched their lives; they became significant in the eyes of God. If we want to be disciples of Jesus, then we will use His gifts wisely. I often ask myself, do I use the gifts God has given me to help others? Is the life I am living pleasing to God?

If I am candid with myself, the answer will be no, because I can never be that perfect and always be the person He wants me to be. Even when we fail, the true disciple keeps his focus on God's purpose; we know the meaning of asking for forgiveness. Being true disciples, regardless of our shortcomings, we keep pushing forward.

1 Peter 5:1-4: "To the elders among you, I appeal as a fellow elder, a witness of Christ's suffering and one who also will share in the glory to be revealed. Be shepherds of God's flock that is under your care, serving as overseers--not because you must, but because you are willing, as God wants you to be; not greedy for money, but eager to serve; not lording it over those entrusted to you, but being examples to the flock. And when the Chief Shepherd appears, you will receive a crown of glory that will never fade away."

Peter was addressing the elders in the church. He is also talking to the people who choose to be God's disciples. The greeter at church is just as crucial as the Pastor. When we leave the church on Sunday morning, we still represent our church. We are the church!

The flocks are people in the church and people God places on our journey. We are overseers; we lead by our example. We are not judgmental, better than them(lording); we treat others with the same understanding and compassion that Jesus gives us.

The real sign of greatness is how we allow God's Spirit to work through us. Many of us will never be rich, but God will measure our greatness(success) when we face Him. God will measure success by the way we lived our lives. Are we forgiving? Do we plant good seeds? We will all meet our Creator; then God will measure success by how we lived our lives, for some will receive a crown of glory that will last an eternity!

CHAPTER 20

Fear of God.

Fear is more than just a word; for many, fear keeps them isolated from others(depression). Fear, for some, keeps us from doing the things God wants us to do. Being fearless doesn't mean we are not afraid.

The fear I talk about is the absence of faith and limiting God's ability to make things different. The fear that keeps us from moving forward or accomplishing God's purpose. Fear of God means knowing the power of God and being in awe of His power. If the fear of God is inside you, you will understand that all power and control are in His hands.

God didn't fight anyone with His fists. His courageous act was to suffer persecution for the sins of humanity. Jesus confronted the haters by forgiving them before He died.

Genesis 15:1: "After this, the word of the LORD came to Abram in a vision: Do not be afraid, Abram, I am your shield, your great reward." God made a promise to Abram(Abraham) that he would be the father of all nations. When we read the stories in the Old Testament, we realize God is faithful. Fear Of God gave people(Old Testament) the courage to face all their concerns. They had a genuine fear of God, knowing He had all the power.

Abraham had to make decisions. He could stay in his homeland or follow God's direction and go where God was leading him. Because of his faith and trust in God, he would become the father of the Jewish nation. God knew what was inside the heart of Abraham; God knew Abraham would be faithful. Throughout the Old Testament, God picked people He knew would trust Him. Even today, God elects people who He knows will be committed to His purpose.

Abraham died at an old age leaving two sons Isaac and Ishmael. Isaac had two sons. Genesis 25:27-34: We learn the story about Esau and Jacob. Esau despised his birthrights; later on, he lost his blessing Isaac gave to the oldest son. With a plan made by his mother, Jacob tricked Isaac into giving Esau's birthrights to Jacob. When Isaac dies, Esau makes a vow to kill Jacob; Jacob flees to Laban out of fear. God would keep His promise to Abraham, and both brothers would prosper.

Genesis 31:3: "Then the LORD said to Jacob, 'Go back to the land of your fathers and to your relative, and I will be with you.'" Laban was a selfish man; he tried to outmaneuver Rebekah(Jacob's wife). But when God has a plan in someone's life, He can overcome any obstacle in His path. Laban lost control of Jacob and his wife. Despite how much Jacob feared going back to his country, he would do what God wanted him to do.

Can you imagine facing someone you hurt in the past, knowing the hurt and pain you caused that person? Jacob prayed to God for His forgiveness, and God saved him from the anger his brother had for him(Genesis 32:11).

The night before he would meet Esau, Jacob fought with God to get His blessing(Genesis 32:22-28). Fear can keep us from doing what we need to do, but having a fear of God's power can give us the courage to follow His commands. Making amends to people you have harmed in the past is part of the freedom to heal the present pains. As long as approaching them wouldn't cause them or yourself harm, God can give everyone the same opportunity He was giving Jacob.

Genesis 33:3-4: "He went on ahead and bowed down to the ground seven times as he approached his brother. But Esau ran to Jacob and embraced him; he threw his arms around his neck and kissed him." Despite the four hundred soldiers he saw with Esau, Jacob faced up to one of his biggest fears.

When we approach people we have harmed in the past, not all our results can be the same as Jacob's. When we start to make amends to people we harmed in the past, some people won't forgive us. The second part of our amendment is to change our behavior and become the person that stops hurting people. Regardless of the results, our life can still move forward.

Exodus 3:11-12: "But Moses said to God, 'Who am I, that I should go to Pharoah and bring the Israelites out of Egypt?' I will be with you. And this will be a sign for you that it is I who sent you. When you brought the people out of Egypt, you will worship God on this mountain."

God gave Moses a mission. Moses had a fear of God, and God's power was more reliable than his fears. When God's Spirit wants us to move, we can be confident that God will give us the strength to accomplish His goals.

When we are in awe of God's power and His glory and how He can change our lives, we have a genuine fear of God. When we believe God created the universe, made man, then we realize God has the power to overcome our fears.

Reading the Book of Job, we begin to understand the power that God wants us to feel. Regardless of the pain Job went through, the sores inflicted on his body, even the depression and despair he often would feel. We begin to realize—the fear of God inside him is more substantial than what the world has given him.

Job 6:8-10: "Oh, that I might have my request, that God would grant what I hope for, that God would be willing to crush me, to let loose His hand and cut off my life! Then I would still have this consolation--my joy in relenting pain--that I had not denied the words of the Holy One." Even when his friends and wife criticize him, he never denied God's presence and power.

Proverbs 1:7: "The fear of the LORD is the beginning of knowledge, but fools despise wisdom and instruction."

My behavior kept me from the joy that only God could give me. After 12 years of using drugs and alcohol and thirty-five years of sobriety, I finally met Jesus Christ and made Him my Savior, and I felt immediate results. The fear of God gave me His power, and with His power inside me, I began to change.

Luke 12:4-5: "I tell you, my friends, do not be afraid of those who kill the body and after that can do no more. But I will show you, Whom you should fear: Fear Him who, after your body has been killed, has authority to throw you into hell. Yes, I tell you, fear Him." Jesus is telling us to fear Him, who has the power to save our souls. God is the author of our soul's life or death.

Jesus was speaking about those who kill the body(church). The Pharisees were killing His church. There are many forms of hypocrisy; one is to speak against the power of God, another is so-called Christians who say they are Christians but live a life opposed to His teachings. The Pharisees are afraid Jesus would take their power away. The way the Pharisees lived their lives opposes the will of Jesus. A genuine person who has a fear of God knows He has all the power!

When people make fun of God, do we hold back and say nothing? Does our fear of what people might think to keep us from speaking out? Does the fear of God motivate me to change into a better person? Does the fear of God save me from sinning?

Luke 12:35-48; Jesus gives us the story and a warning that He is coming back. He speaks to the apostles in a parable about the master leaving two slaves in charge of his home. The one is wise and faithful, while the other is a drinker who thinks I can do anything I want. Verse 46: "The Master of that servant will come on a day when he does not expect Him, and at an hour he is not aware of. He will cut him to pieces and assign him a place with the unbelievers." We never know the hour when we will meet our Savior. If that moment happened today, would you be ready?

Verse 47: "That servant who knows his Master's will and does not get ready or does not do what the Master wants will be beaten with many blows." Verse 48: "But the one that does not know and does things deserving punishment will be beaten with fewer blows. From everyone who has been given much, much will be demanded; and from the one that is entrusted with much, much more will be asked."

Many people don't care about God and live a life as opposed to all His' teachings. Some are reasonable people and try living a good life; God is fair and treats them kindly. Then come the people who have much; God expects more from them. Ultimately God will judge each person.

Many churches don't preach this message; maybe they are afraid of losing people, but what happens to our souls when we die is a big part of God's word to all of us. Even if we don't believe in heaven or hell doesn't matter; we will all be there one day.

I know the power of God by the changes He has made in my life. Jesus is accurate, and I have a fear of His power. I feel excited when I realize this life we live is preparing me for the time I spend with God. Ultimately God will judge me by what He sees inside my soul!

Feeling Defeated

Can you imagine what Moses went through when the Israelites would rebel? Time after time, he would go to God utterly defeated and plead to God to forgive the Israelites. The prophets had to take so much abuse while prophesying. Despite the cruelty of the people and how they felt defeated at times, they still spoke out God's word. The feeling of being upset(defeated) isn't new to Christians throughout the world. Feeling defeated is part of the world; being disciples, we can always find comfort, knowing God is still in control.

"You, dear children, are from God and have overcome them, because the One who is in you is greater than the one who is in the world(1 John4:4.) Feeling defeated is part of the world we live in; Satan(he) uses times when we are weak, telling us the world is in control. Regardless of the world's vanity and arrogance, people are making Jesus their Lord and Savior. When we pick up our cross and truly repent; the Holy Spirit starts to live within us.

In the world today, people are lonely, depressed, and in some cases, because of the conditions they are living in, they are oppressed. In many parts of the world, people still can't worship God freely. One of my friends and his wife were put in jail, trying to bring Bibles into North Korea. By the grace of God and their faith, they were allowed to come home. This happened to them years ago; now, the Bible is in different languages throughout the world. Regardless of what the government tries to control, Jesus is finding a home to live in!

Psalms 9:7-10: "The LORD reigns forever. He has established His throne for judgment. He will judge the world in righteousness; He will govern the people with justice. The LORD is a refuge for the oppressed, a stronghold in times of trouble. Those who know your name will trust in You, for You, LORD, have never forsaken those who seek You."

David wrote this Psalm after having victory in a battle against the Philistines. David would always pray before and after going into battle. Even when he was oppressed or feeling success, he knew enough to seek God and pray. We live in a different world than Davids, but we still have the same God.

Psalm 42:1-2: "As a deer pants for streams of water, so my soul pants for You, O God. My soul thirsts for God, for the living God. When can I go and meet with God?"

Korah was a Levite who led a rebellion against David. He was killed in a battle against David, but some of his sons survived. David made them choir directors. They would get lonely and depressed while meditating on God's goodness and love; they wrote Psalm 42. While praying, God would give them hope. These people poured out their hearts to God. When reading these Psalms, we are pouring out our feelings and asking God to help us.

Psalm 42:5-6: "Why are you downcast, O my soul? Why so disturbed within me? Put your hope in God, for I will yet praise Him, my Savior, and my God." When discouraged or depressed, they would meditate on God's goodness. Many times all we can do is pray. When we meditate and read these Psalms, they bring our focus back to God and the hope that only He can give us.

Proverbs 29:23: "A man's pride brings him low, but a man of lowly spirit gains honor." Sometimes we can get so caught up in the world around us, and we forget to do the things that keep us grounded. When the world around me becomes more important than my relationship with God, I feel out of balance. Many times our pride is excellent, and we won't ask anyone to help us. Hitting bottom emotionally, I finally ask God to help me.

Isaiah 51:12-13a: "I, even I, am He who comforts you. Who are you that you fear mortal men, the sons of men, who are but grass, that you forget the LORD your Maker, Who stretched out the heavens and laid the foundations of the earth."

Isaiah was telling them to trust God and the principles God was trying to instill into their spirit. The people were in fear of Babylon and how they would rule them. God had power over anything that would happen. Isaiah wanted the people to fear God, who had more power than the Babylonians. To fear God is to be in awe of His power. When I feel defeated, what do I fear? What is my Babylon? Instead of feeling defeat, shouldn't I try to focus on God and His power?

Matthew 5:3: "Blessed are the poor in spirit, for theirs is the kingdom of heaven." When Jesus gave us His first sermon, this was how it started. There are ways of doing things that can help us. It all started because many of us were poor in spirit and broken. It began by reaching out to God for help. Depression and loneliness are part of the world we live in, but because of God's Spirit inside us, we have the power to change those feelings. If you have a personal relationship with God, you are never alone!

Matthew 10:28: "Do not be afraid of those who kill the body but cannot kill the soul. Rather, be afraid of the One who can destroy both soul and body in hell." The soul of man is eternal; Jesus came to free our souls.

Verses 29-31: "Are not two sparrows sold for a penny? Yet none of them will fall to the ground apart from the will of your Father. And even the hairs of your head are numbered. So don't be afraid; you are worth more than many sparrows." When talking to the apostles, Jesus was warning them about persecution. He was telling them not to worry. He would take care of them. Persecution because of religious beliefs, especially because of race or political views. At times in our life, we will all face forms of persecution.

Even though we are spirit-filled Christians, we will lose contact with God's Spirit inside us. God always has a picture of what will happen in our life. Often, the key to success is doing the right things that will lead us back to God—making decisions with God's guidance, keeping close to my friends, and asking them for help.

How long does it take before I ask my friends to help me? How often do I suffer because I am silent?

Romans 8:36-39: "As it is written: For your sake, we face death all day long: we are considered as sheep to be slaughtered. No, in all these things we are more than conquerors through Him who loved us. For I am convinced that neither death nor life, neither angels nor demons, neither the present nor the future, nor any powers, neither height nor depth, nor anything else in all creation, will be able to separate us from the love of God that is in Christ Jesus our Lord."

We can get caught up in the world, and we become a victim of being human. Sometimes we can get to the point of despair. Even at times like this, God is working inside you to make things better. So we persevere and try not to lose heart; we know God is stronger than the obstacles that have gotten in our way. Paul was warning the Roman Church that they would face persecution. He was telling them the power of God would heal and protect them. Regardless of what would happen, nothing could separate them from God and His strength.

2 Corinthians 12:7-10: "To keep me from being conceited because of these great revelations, there was given to me a thorn on my flesh, a messenger of Satan, to torment me. Three times I pleaded with the Lord to take it away from me. But He said to me, 'My grace is sufficient for you, for my power is made perfect in weakness.' Therefore I will boast all the more gladly about my weaknesses, so that Christ's power may rest on me. That is why, for Christ's sake, I delight in weaknesses, in insult, in hardship, in persecution, in difficulties. For when I am weak, then I am strong."

Paul didn't tell us what the thorn in his side was, but we can be blessed knowing God is always stronger than our weaknesses. Many times when we feel weak, God is building character. God wants us to challenge any defect, knowing God's grace is more potent. There will be times when we have to face defeat. Getting through these times has made me stronger(developed character). When we have difficult times, God wants us to draw close to Him!

Fellowship

Acts 20:31: "So be on your guard! Remember that for three years I never stopped warning each of you night and day with tears." Paul was making a farewell speech to the Ephesian Elders. Verse 34-35: "You yourselves know that these hands of mine have supplied my own needs and the needs of my companions." Paul was a tentmaker; much of his trips are supplied by money he made.

"In everything I did, I showed you that by this kind of hard work we must help the weak, remembering the words the Lord Jesus himself said: 'It is more blessed to give than to receive.'" Paul gives us an excellent example of sharing and fellowship. Paul's life wouldn't have any meaning or purpose if he could not share this gift. For me to keep what God has given me, I need to give it away.

Romans 6:5-7: "For if we are united with Him in a death like his, we will certainly also be united with Him in His resurrection. For we know our old self was crucified with Him that the body ruled by sin might be done away with, that we should no longer be slaves to sin-- because anyone who has died has been set free from sin."

What happens to us when we have fellowship with Jesus? If we have fellowship with God, our old Spirit will become a part of His death, and our new self becomes a part of His resurrection.

Having fellowship with Jesus, we no longer are slaves to sin. Being a part of the world, we still can sin, and sometimes we will. The difference is that we choose how we want to live; we no longer are slaves to sin. My old self was crucified with Christ; having fellowship with Jesus has given me a new life.

The life I live in the body, I live by faith in the Son of God, who loved me and gave Himself for me(Galatians 2:20.)" The focus of the Christian life is not about dying; having fellowship with Jesus has given me eternal life. "God, who has called you into fellowship with his Son Jesus Christ our Lord, is faithful(1 Cor 1:9.)"

"Those who obey His commands live in him, and He in them. And this is how we know that He lives in us: We know it by the Spirit He gave us(1 John 3:24.)" To have fellowship with Christ, we need to follow three basic principles: (1) believe in Christ. (2) Love your brothers and sisters. (3) Live moral lives.

Hebrews 10:23-25: "Let us hold unswervingly to the hope we profess, for He who promised is faithful. And let us consider how we can spur one another on toward love and good deeds. Let us not give up meeting together, as some are in the habit of doing, but encouraging one another-- and all the more as you see the day approaching."

Jesus wants us to meet and bond together. Part of God's command is to love your brother and sisters. The day is approaching talks about when God will come back to the world a second time. Regardless of when that time comes, we need to get right with God.

Philippians 1:7-8: "It is right for me to feel this way about you since I have you in my heart, and whether I am in chains or defending and confirming the gospel, all of you share in God's grace with me. God can testify how I long for you with the affection of Jesus Christ."

Even while he was in prison, Paul had a bond with us. It was God's purpose and the Holy Spirit inside him that wouldn't allow him to give up. By writing these letters to the churches and us who believe, he could encourage us and keep him from losing hope.

Verse 8: "God can testify how I long for you with the affection of Jesus Christ." Jesus Christ binds all of our lives together. The Holy Spirit joins us and makes us one. That is why when we have fellowship Christ is there amongst us. Paul wanted to show us how to handle suffering. His perseverance and his courage show me, I too, can handle adversity. God inspired people(anointed) to write the Bible, reading the Bible every day I can have fellowship with the words God has written!

1 John 1:3-4: "We proclaim what we have seen and heard, so that you may have fellowship with us. And our fellowship is with the Father and with His Son, Jesus Christ. We write this to make our joy complete."

Having fellowship with fellow Christians keeps our joy complete. There are times when we want to run and hide, but these are times when we need connection with one another. When I get away from going to church or missing my Bible studies, my life gets out of balance. When I don't listen to the Holy Spirit telling me to do something, I miss out on a blessing.

Three principles happen when I stay connected to the church and my Bible studies: (1) Our fellowship is grounded by God's word. (2) Our unity is mutual, and we can share our faith. (3) Our hope and strength are being renewed. Church and Bible studies keep us grounded. God didn't want us to walk this world alone. That is why fellowship with God and fellow Christians is so important!

Finances

The world is on shut down; we are dealing with Coronavirus (Covid-19). Many right now are in a financial crisis. What a time to talk about finances!

I am praying God will step in, and they can find a cure. I am thankful; I have a God who can give me comfort. Even when it seems the world is falling apart, this is when He gives me hope. I know that I can draw close to God and learn some lessons.

Proverbs 18:11: "The wealth of the rich is their fortified city; they imagine it an unscalable wall." People who put their power in their money think their wealth is unscalable. Ecclesiastes 10:19: "A feast is made for laughter, and wine makes life merry, but money is the answer for everything." Life is excellent; the more money we make, the happier we feel.

After a while, the wine gets warm, and it becomes bitter. The stock market has gone from 28,000 points to the most significant loss in two days, 19,000. The Coronavirus has put the stock market in a downward cycle. The world is in a shutdown.

Ecclesiastes 1:2-3: "Meaningless! Meaningless! Says the Teacher. Utterly meaningless! Everything is meaningless. What does a man gain from all his labor at which he toils under the sun?" Looking at the stock market, I don't have much, but I ask myself, what good was it saving money? My thoughts go to the world and how many people come to this conclusion. A Failed marriage, losing everything you owned, maybe a sudden illness(accident), this is a time when we can feel our life has become meaningless.

" We know in all things God works for the good of those who love Him, who have been called according to His purpose,(Romans 8:28.)"

What good is happening when everything seems like it is falling apart? At times like this, I ask myself, what do I put my value on? Times like these can make me question God.

Ecclesiastes 1:15-16: "What is twisted cannot be straightened; what is lacking cannot be counted. I thought to myself, I have grown and increased in wisdom more than anyone who has ruled over Jerusalem before me; I have experienced much of wisdom and knowledge." Solomon wanted wisdom; people came from near and far to hear his wisdom. Solomon was a teacher; he devoted his life to exploring understanding.

Verse 18, he seems to question everything He has learned about wisdom: "For with much wisdom comes sorrow; the more knowledge, the more grief." I have been a Christian for many years. I have devoted my life to following Jesus. With all the wisdom God has given me, I still feel grief and loss. The Coronavirus is destroying the knowledge God has given me.

The world I built around me crashed down; all the wisdom I thought I had seemed meaningless. Looking at verse 18, I begin to understand what Solomon was saying. Human knowledge can lead to answers, but I wouldn't have any answers without Jesus in my life. Without Jesus in my life, my wisdom only causes me grief!

Ecclesiastes 2:10: "I denied nothing my eyes desired; I refused my heart no pleasure. My heart took delight in all my work. and this was the reward for all my labor." Looking at this verse, I realize how little I have given up on my journey and how my pride has given me a sense of achievement, how I didn't deny myself any of the pleasures of this world I created.

Verse 11: "Yet when I surveyed all that my hands have done and what I had toiled to achieve, everything was meaningless, a chasing after the wind; nothing was gained under the sun." Solomon was beginning to understand what God was telling him? Maybe God was talking to me and asking me, "What do you put your worth on?"

So in verses 17-18, he uses hate when talking about toil: "So, I hated life, because the work that is done under the sun was grievous to me. All of it meaningless, a chasing after the wind." I hated all the things I have toiled for under the sun because I must leave them to the one who comes after me." You can never outrun the wind; it just keeps blowing. You can't take your wealth with you after you die. Without God in his life, it would have no meaning!

Verse 24 He comes to a realization: "A man can do nothing better than to eat and drink and find satisfaction in his work. This, too, I see, is from God's hand, for without Him, who can eat and find enjoyment?" Solomon begins to realize, God is the source of his joy!

We often fight with the world and God's presence in our lives, and I forget my world would mean nothing without God. Then in a gentle voice, the Holy Spirit was talking to me. We can't compare this world to the one Solomon would rule centuries ago. The challenges we face are different, but the one thing that remains the same is God. The truth about money and the value we place on our pride never changes. The truth about money and how much cost we place on possessions never varies.

The Holy Spirit was telling me something, and I began to hear what He was saying. He wants us to realize how this world puts so much value on money and possessions. Money isn't the source of evil; it's the value that we place on money.

At this moment, I realize God will provide. God's love and promises will never change. I begin to cry; I understand all this is meaningless; the only thing that has any meaning is God. I know all we have can fade away, but God will still provide and take care of me!

Finances 2

After being filled with the Holy Spirit, my opinions on church and finance began to change. I knew finding a good church is essential. I began to realize I have a responsibility for how I handle my money. Let me take a moment to say, "God doesn't need our money." Even if we don't have any money, God can use the gifts He has given us.

I started giving small amounts to the church, but God touched my heart, and I started giving to other organizations. I received the greatest gift because I didn't worry about finances; I knew God would provide if I used my money wisely.

I did a personal study on finance, and three things stood out: 1. Giving and tithing are essential in my life. 2. I couldn't worship money and place it above God. 3. When I do give from the heart, God will always give me what I need. I learned we could never out-give what God can provide. The more I gave, the more He can trust me to handle. God constantly challenges me to give more!

Jeremiah 9:23-24: "This is what the LORD says: Let not the wise man boast of his wisdom or the strong man boast of his strength or the rich man boast about his riches, but let him who boasts boast about this: that he understands and knows Me, that I am LORD, Who exercises kindness, justice, and righteousness on earth, for these I delight."

We can't buy our way into God's heart! What matters to God is how we use what He has given us. What matters to God is our words and if they lead into action. Through Jeremiah and his prophecies, I learn what God expects from me.

Malachi 3:8-10: "Will a wise man rob God? Yet you rob Me, but you ask, 'How do I rob You?' In tithes and offerings. You are under a curse--the whole nation of you because you are robbing Me. Bring the whole tithe into the warehouse, that there might be food in My house. Test Me in this, says the LORD Almighty, and see If I will not throw open the floodgates of heaven and pour out so much blessing that you will not have enough room for it." God is challenging us to give more; when we do things for the right reasons, God will always bless us.

God had the power to give or to take away. The people in the Old Testament hadn't received the baptism of the Holy Spirit, so God spoke to them using His prophets. What they learned and spoke through them(prophets) was passed unto us. Tithing was the standard God used when He asked them for their help.

Without our tithing, our churches can't run. God is working through many of the organizations that we as Christians support. God doesn't want our families to suffer, but if the Holy Spirit tells us to give, we are capable and can afford to give.

Matthew 6:19-21: "Do not store up for yourselves treasures on earth, where moth and rust destroy, and where thieves break in and steal. But store up for yourselves treasures in heaven, where moth and rust do not destroy, and where thieves do not break in and steal. For where your heart is, there your heart will also be." I think to myself," Do I allow money and possessions to rob me of the joy only God can give me?

Verse 24, the Holy Spirit is teaching us: "No man can serve two masters. Either he will hate the one and love the other, or he will be devoted to the one and despise the other. You cannot serve God and money." We can store up money and be secure at the moment. For some, holding on to capital becomes more important than giving God what He deserves.

I learned a lesson a long time ago about possessions. I remember how an operation on my hand and wrist failed, and I lost all the feeling in one of my arms. I learned how properties mean nothing without the use of my arm. It would take a full year of therapy three times a week, and I gained back the use of my arm.

God showed me the trap of materialism, how money had become the root of all my happiness. The more I made meant I could spend more, looking back, "Did I gain anything?" Money robbed my family of the time I could spend with them. Our children don't need more money; they need quality time. Making more money in many ways became the root of evil.

Mark 4:18-19: "Still others, like seed sown among thorns, hear the word; but the worries of this life, the deceitfulness of wealth and the desire for other things come in and choke the word, making it unfruitful." One of the reasons we fall away from God is what we place our values around. God wants our lives to have a balance.

Philippians 4:10-13: "I rejoice greatly in the Lord that at last, you have renewed your concerns for me. Indeed you have been concerned, but you had no opportunity to show it." In this verse, Paul is thanking the church for helping him. But he follows it up by saying: "I am not saying this because I am in need, for I have learned to be content whatever the circumstances." Paul looked toward God to give him what he needed. He learned to be content with plenty or when he didn't have anything. Verse 13: " I can do everything through Him Who gives me strength." Paul knew God was the source of all his power. He also knew the joy God gave him in good or bad times!

1 Timothy 6:10: "For the love of money is the root of all kinds of evil. Some people. eager for money, have wandered from the faith, and pierced themselves with many griefs." Once again, I can look at money differently. I am learning how to be content with plenty or not having enough. The bottom line; God doesn't need our money unless we give it graciously. God knows our hearts, and when we are gracious, He will continue blessing us in many ways!

Forgiveness

Matthew 5:21; "You have heard that it was said to the people long ago. Do not murder, and anyone that murders will be subject to judgment." God uses murder to show us what happens to a person with a sinful heart. A person with an unforgiving heart can pass judgment on themselves.

Our past, a friend's betrayal, divorce, all those things can cause us anger. We were not being promoted at work, not getting the attention we deserve, even false pride, basing our life around accomplishments, and then watching them fade away.

Getting older, sickness, some of the choices we made, even losing someone in a tragic accident all these things can lead to anger. God doesn't condone violence in any form, but you can be a victim of another's insanity. If we don't deal with our passion, it can turn to unforgiveness; in many cases, unforgiveness can destroy people's lives.

Verse 22a: "But I tell you that anyone angry with his brother will be subject to judgment." What happens when we seek justice and the thought of vengeance consumes our spirit? What happens to God's joy when we hold on to anger? Anger is part of the grieving process, but we become a subject of anger when we hold on to the violence.

Verse 22b: "Again, anyone who says to his brother, Raca, is answerable to the Sanhedrin. But anyone that says, 'You fool!' will be in danger of the fire of hell." Raca comes from the Arabic term reqa; it's an offensive term used to show utter contempt for another. In the ancient land of Israel, hatred could be considered a crime. The Sanhedrin would settle these disagreements. This group of men was the judge and jury. If they found you guilty, people could stone you to death in a public place.

Killing someone is a horrible sin, and God commands us to love our brothers and sisters. When we forgive someone who trespasses against us, we can move forward. When we are unforgiving, we are still bound to that person. By being forgiving, we're not saying what they did was right. Forgiveness gives us the ability to move forward. People live a lifetime of being angry; they become a subject of their anger. They no longer have the ability to move forward. We truly punish ourselves by holding on to anger.

Matthew 6:14-15: "For if you forgive men when they sin against you, your heavenly Father will also forgive you. But if you do not forgive men their sins, your Father will not forgive you." God knew how unforgiveness could destroy a person; that was why He wants us to forgive others.

Matthew 18:21-22: "Then Peter came to Jesus and asked, 'Lord, how many times shall I forgive my brother when he sins against me?' Up to seven times?" Jesus answered, 'I tell you, not seven times, but seventy-seven times.'" The bottom line, unforgiveness will hurt us!

In a small Mississippi town, a gunman went into a church and started shooting. Following what happened, the people came out and publicly forgave the shooter. Their forgiveness took an action that shouldn't have happened, and some good came out of this tragedy. Because of their mercy, they could bury and mourn the loss of their loved ones. Their actions were not saying what the gunman did was right, but their forgiveness helped them move on. They set an example that all Christians throughout the world should follow.

In the Old Testament, we read the story about Joseph, the youngest of Jacob's 12 children. His brothers were jealous of him, so they made a plan to kill him. Instead of killing him, they left him in a hole in the desert. Despite all the suffering he went through, Joseph had a forgiving heart. Through all his pain, He would remain faithful to God. In Genesis, you read about Joseph and his life(Genesis 37:1-50.)

While on his journey, he ended up interpreting a dream for Pharoah. Pharoah ended up giving him a high position in his government. Joseph ended up interpreting another dream, and he would build a building to store wheat, preparing Egypt for the famine that he saw coming in the dream.

Jacob needed wheat to get through the famine, so he sent all his older sons to Joseph. They didn't recognize Joseph as their brother. Eventually, he would tell them.

Genesis 50:19-21: "Joseph said to them, 'Don't be afraid, am I in the place of God?' You intended to harm me, but God intended it for good to accomplish what now is being done, the saving of many lives. So then, don't be afraid, I will provide for you and your children. And he reassured them and spoke kindly."

I can see how good came out of evil for those who trust in God. Joseph had a forgiving heart, and he kept his eyes on God. When we hold on to anger, it can turn to resentment and self-pity. Joseph didn't allow his anger to destroy God's plan.

Acts 7:55-56: "Steven filled with the Holy Spirit, looked up to heaven and saw the glory of God, and Jesus was standing at the right hand of God. Look, he said, 'I see heaven open and the Son of the man standing at the right hand of God.'"

In verses 59-60, he continues praying: "While they were stoning him, Stephen prayed, 'Lord Jesus, receive my spirit.' Then he fell to his knees and cried out, 'Lord do not hold this sin against them.'" While being stoned, Stephen would ask God to forgive the people that were stoning him.

Luke 23:33-34: "When they came to a place called the Skull, they crucified Him(Jesus) there, along with the criminals-one on His right, the other on His left. Jesus said, 'Father forgive them, for they know not what they are doing.'" Forgiveness, Jesus was setting an example for us to follow.

People can live a life of being angry. Jesus came to set us free. Forgiving the people who harmed me and forgiving myself because of the hurt I caused others helped me move forward. God had a future planned for me. Having a forgiving heart, I could begin this journey.

Philippians 2:3-4: "Do nothing out of selfish ambition or vain conceit, but in humility, consider others better than yourself. Each of you should look not only to your interests but also to the interests of others."

Paul suffered persecution daily. Instead of getting angry, he wrote letters to the different churches. The world says, "He had every right to be angry, but Paul knew anger would destroy God's Spirit inside him. God used his passion in the right way; Paul would write thirty percent of the New Testament. Even though he was inside a prison, his life was moving forward!

Hope: Hard Times

Parents are losing kids because of the anger in the world today. Homicide is the top result of a death in children 5-18 years old. The divorce percentage for first-year marriages is forty to fifty percent. For second and third marriages, 65 to 75 percent are failing. When we talk to people who experience loss, how can we help them?

Living in this world, we will have struggles. Things happen that shouldn't happen; even bad things happen to good people. Sickness, the pandemic virus, death all these conditions are part of the world. All people will experience depression, betrayal, unnecessary deaths at certain times; Regardless of what is going on, God can give us His hope.

Job 6:8-10: "Oh, that I might have my request, that God could grant what I hope for, that God would be willing to crush me, to let loose His hand and cut off my life! Then I would still have this consolation--my joy in relenting pain--that I had not denied the words of the Holy One."

When Job felt so much despair, he hoped he wouldn't deny the words of the Holy One. Deep down, he knew God wasn't doing these things to him.

Job(Book of Job) suffered loneliness and despair, sickness, and judgment from his friends, not even his wife's support. Despite all his pain, he never denied the presence of God. He never blamed God for all the suffering he was going through. God knew what lay inside Job's heart; that was why He allowed the devil to torment him. In the end, God gave Job even more than what he had. When we go through trying times, who knows what lies on the other side?

There will be times when we feel lost in our Christian journey, and God seems so far away. Even though the Holy Spirit is inside us, we can feel empty. Irrespective of how you think or feel, God is always giving you the strength to move forward.

Psalms 3:1-3: "O LORD, how many are my foes! How many rise up against me! Many are saying, 'God will not deliver him.' But you, Lord, are my shield around me, my glory, the one who lifts my head high." David was running from his son and some traitors; instead of letting fear get the best of him, he trusts God would lead him in the right direction. David knew his only hope was in God, guiding him in the right direction. This is the same hope God wants us to develop!

When hope seems far away, even as true believers, we can question God. Instead of challenging God, we should reach out and ask Him for help. Instead of pulling away, this is a time that God wants to draw us closer.

Jeremiah 29:11: "For I know the plans I have for you, 'declares the LORD,' plans to prosper you and not to harm you, plans to give you hope and a future." God used Jeremiah as his prophet. As prophesied in the Old Testament, the Babylonians would take over.

The Israelites started to worship other gods. Through God's discipline, they learned to worship the one true God. Many would repent and return to Him. The Israelites were allowed to stay together. They settled in towns along the Chebar River. They would farm, and some of them became wealthy. After the Persians defeated the Babylonians, they were allowed to go back to Jerusalem. With the Help of Ezra, they would start to rebuild the temple. God planned to draw the people back to Him!

When God seems far away, He has a policy for those who put their faith in Him. The plan can lead to getting something better. When it seems all is lost, God gives us hope and the courage to keep moving forward; The discipline and perseverance to keep our eyes on God. When everything seems out of our control, God gives us the knowledge that He is still in control.

Mark 5:35: "While speaking, some men came from the house of Jairus, the synagogue ruler. 'Your daughter is dead,' they said. Why bother, the Teacher, anymore?"

Verse 36 Jesus would ignore what they said; "Jesus told the synagogue ruler, 'Don't be afraid, just believe.'" We know Jesus went to his home and would raise Jarius's daughter from the dead. What can we learn? When everything seems out of control, "just believe." Jesus is the source of our hope; when all hope seems lost," believe!"

Romans 5:3-4: "Not only so, but we rejoice in our suffering because we know that suffering produces perseverance; perseverance, character; and character, hope." I never knew character building would lead to hope. Perseverance is a character-building that can keep our faith in us and give us strength. Regardless of the situations around us, determination(discipline) keeps our focus on Jesus. Keeping our focus on Jesus keeps the hope inside us alive!

Verse 5 He goes on by saying: "And hope does not disappoint us, because God has poured out His love into our hearts, by the Holy Spirit, whom He has given us." Hope lies in the Holy Spirit that God has put in us. God's promise is living inside us(Holy Spirit) even while going through hard times that Spirit is working and giving us hope.

Romans 8:24: "For in hope we were saved. Now hope that is not seen is not hope. For who hopes for what he sees?" In verse 25, Jesus reminds us: "But if we hope for what we do not see, we wait for it with patience." Then in verse 28, Jesus gives us a promise: "And we know for those who love God all things work together for good, for those who are called according to His purpose."

1 Peter 5:10-11: "And the God of all grace, who called you to His eternal glory in Christ, after you have suffered a little while, will Himself restore you and make you strong, firm and steadfast. To Him be the power forever and ever. Amen."

2020 has been a year of acceptance, unable to change many of the things that have happened. It was a year of sadness; many lost loved ones and close friends. At the peak of the pandemic, many lost business that they worked hard to maintain. For me, I realized how this world could change in a moment. We all suffered, but those who believe in Jesus would get more substantial. Peter talks about God's grace, even after we suffered a while, will make us stronger.

For some who don't believe in God, they would meet Jesus. For some whose faith was weak, we would gain a more vital trust. This year we learned about our differences and the prejudice many of us carry in our hearts. For some, it was a time to try understanding why anyone would vote for that person. There were riots, and never has the United States been so divided in their differences. Groups took advantage of America at our weakest time!

God wants Christians to keep a united front; we can have our differences(politically) but remain united in what we believe. Regardless of our circumstances, we know God is in control. God gives us an understanding of what the world thinks. God provides us with the ability to look at others and their circumstances. God shows us what is essential in our lives and what is vital on our journey. As Christians, we can rise above the hate and allow people the right to voice their opinions. At all times, we try to be peaceful and calm!

As Christians, regardless of who we voted for, we can remain faithful to God and what He teaches us. It's a time to share the love and compassion Jesus put inside my heart and help others. It's a time for Christians to pray and ask God to heal this nation!

Humility

Exodus 3:11: "But Moses said to God, 'Who am I, that I should go to Pharoah and bring the Israelites out of Egypt?'" Here was a man who used to be an Egyptian prince and was thrown out of his country. He became a Midianite shepherd; now, God asked him to go back to Egypt and deliver His people out of slavery. What a humbling experience Moses had to be feeling. Being humbled, he had to be committed to God to fulfill God's purpose.

DO YOU KNOW THE TRUTH?

We know the story about David and how he had to face Goliath. David was one of God's favorite people; before doing anything, he would pray to God and ask for guidance. He was a humble man who would lead many people into battle. He stood up to Saul(King of Israel), who was jealous of his attention. David became a great King and wrote many of the Psalms in the Book of Psalms.

Psalms 8:3-5: "When I consider Your heavens, the work of Your fingers, the moon, and the stars that You have set in place, what is a man that You are mindful of him, the son of man that You care for him? You made him a little lower than the heavenly beings and crowned him with glory and honor."

David knew God created everything in the universe; he put man just below the angels and gave him glory and honor. David was in awe of God's power and how insignificant he was in the world. David was a powerful man in the world but knew he was small compared to God, who was all-powerful. He knew all failure or success lay in the hands of God.

Psalms 131:3: "O Israel put your hope in the LORD both now and forever." David knew Israel's trust and contentment could only come from the LORD. He was humble enough to put the people's faith in God's hands. He knew the only way the people would learn to be content was to seek and do God's will.

True humility means I don't have all the answers. It means reaching out to others, knowing I don't have all the answers. Being humble, we always pray to God and seek His advice. We know that He is Lord above all things; We make decisions that profit Him.

True humility means I am teachable. I listen to people before I react or judge them. True humility gives me the willingness to change. Before making major decisions, I go to God and pray. True humility gives me the ability to see others and myself through God's eyes. If I am truly humbled, I can admit to God and others what I did wrong. Meditation shows me how I can change and handle situations differently.

James 4:1-3: "What causes fights and quarrels amongst you? Don't they come from your desires that battle within you? You want something and don't get it. You kill and covet, but you can't have what you want. You quarrel and fight. You do not have because you don't ask God. When you ask, you do not receive, because you ask with wrong motives, that you may spend what you get on your pleasure."

At times I don't get some of the things I want, and I become rebellious. I can go to God with my wants, but many of those wants don't serve God's purpose; they help our pleasure. Being humble(teachable), I know that God can give me what I need. "You do not have because you don't ask God;" the humble person knows how God can give them what they need. When I ask Him for something that I want, I know it's God will be done, not mine!

True humility means stepping back and learning to listen. Instead of reacting and having the last word, God could be teaching me to hear. God puts people in our life for a reason; the humble person learns to listen to what God is trying to say. God gives us an understanding of others and how we can help them. Many times an experience means not saying anything. The person who has true humility knows he can avoid arguments!

James 4:4-6: "You adulteries people, don't you know that friendship with the world is hatred toward God? Anyone who chooses to be a friend of the world becomes an enemy of God. Or do you think Scripture says without reason that the Spirit He causes to live in us envies intensely? But He gives us more grace. That is why Scripture says: God opposes the proud but gives grace to the humble."

The habits we develop or the value we place on what is essential can oppose what God tries to teach us. When the world becomes more important than our relationship with God and His purpose, we commit adultery. How can God help a proud person who has all the answers? When we seek to do God's will in all our affairs, God gives us His grace and mercy!

Philippians 2:3-5: "Do nothing out of selfish ambition, or vain conceit, but in humility, consider others better than yourselves. Each of you should not only look only to your interests but also to the interest of others. Your attitude should be the same as Jesus Christ."

It isn't easy changing, but with God's help, all things are possible. Change takes time and patience. Having humility, God shows me what I need to change and how doing things in the past would hurt me.

Philippians 2:6-8: "Who, being in very nature of God, did not consider equality with God something to be grasped but made Himself nothing, taking the very nature of a servant, being made in human likeness. And being found in the appearance of a man, He humbled Himself and became obedient to death, even death on the cross!"

Jesus humbled Himself before God and humanity. Instead of being like God, He took on the nature of a servant. Jesus showed us His humility. By taking on a man's life, He could understand some of the problems; we have to face. Jesus showed us the way to eternal freedom. Having humility(teachability) helps us to seek and try some of His ways.

1 Corinthians 15:9-10: "For I am the least of the apostles and do not deserve to be an apostle, because I persecuted the Church of God. But by the grace of God, I am what I am, and His grace to me was not without effect. No, I work harder than all of them, yet not I, but the grace of God that was with me."

Paul persecuted Christians that believed in Jesus. Look at how he changed. He admits not evolving on his own, but God's grace changed him. Through Paul's suffering, the Holy Spirit in him can give us hope. Paul knew the true meaning of being humble; Paul knew the head of all his strength was God!

I came to God because the situation in my life was causing me so much pain and heartache. I had no one to turn to except myself, and I no longer had any answers. From the beginning of creation, God knew that humanity would make choices, and many of those choices would lead to being humbled. Nothing makes God happier when people come back and ask Him for help!

CHAPTER 21

Illness

Illness is part of our world; God didn't create this condition, and many of us will experience its effects. When sickness affects our soul, then we get sicker. Knowing God can heal people gives me hope. I have watched people in the fourth stage of cancer, and their faith in God is making them secure. Instead of wanting our pity, they set an example of how we should live. In good or bad times, I like the same Spirit to live in me.

Psalm 27:13: "I am still confident of this; I will see the goodness of the LORD in the land of the living." The land of the living is our life and how it relates to God. Regardless of what we are going through, God will show us His goodness. God never said that we wouldn't get sick. For those who believe in Him, God's Spirit is still inside you and fighting. Complaining and fighting His Spirit can only make things worst. God healing us doesn't mean we will heal completely; at times, healing involves the strength to face whatever happens.

Psalms 73:26: "My flesh and heart may fail, but God is the strength of my heart and my portion forever." Asaph is declaring his confidence in God's presence. When we are sick, we can maintain the presence of God and His ability to make us stronger.

Asaph was the temple choir leader; when he saw any injustice around him, he would keep his hope in the lasting rewards of righteous people. Regardless of our feelings, God always gives us the promise of a resurrected body, one that is free from any sickness.

Good things can happen even when our circumstances seem hopeless. I see people who rise above their circumstances and continue touching the lives of people who know God. Watching them, I am grateful for all the things I can take for granted. Asaph saw the world and all the injustice, but God gave him the strength and wisdom to rise above the earth.

Psalms 91:1-2: "He who dwells in the shelter of the highest will rest in the shadow of the Almighty. I will say of the LORD, 'He is my refuge and my fortress, my God, in whom I trust.'" This author knows putting his trust in God will carry him or her through anything he has to face in his life.

Verses 5-6: 'You will not fear the terror of night, nor the arrow that flies by day, nor the pestilence that stalks in the darkness nor the plague that destroys at midday."

I often get up in the morning and meditate on God's word. Then I start looking at some of the papers I am writing. The first paper I pick up talks about the illness. We are going through a Pandemic virus in our country. The Coronavirus has killed over 3000 lives in Michigan alone, and the hospitals can't handle the flow of people coming in for help. Our government (world) is being shut down because of this Pandemic virus. Reading the verses in Psalm 91 gives me comfort when the world seems like it is falling apart.

Isaiah 40:30-31: "Even youths grow tired and weary, and young people stumble and fall: but those who hope in the LORD will renew their strength. They will soar on wings like eagles; they will run and not grow weary, they will walk and not be faint." I put my hope in God. Regardless of what I hear on the news, I still know God is in control!

Our Governor has told us to stay in our homes. I pray for the people who are sick and the people surrounding them. I pray for the first responders and the doctors and nurses in the hospital. My part is to stay at home and pray. It's times like these when I am so grateful God is part of my life. I can call people I know, showing them some of God's love and support.

Jesus healed me in many ways, but it wasn't a sickness that needed healing. The way I was thinking and living my life was killing me eternally. Jesus can take a mind lost and create a miracle. It isn't the illness that can kill us; it's the destination that keeps our soul in bondage. Regardless of our mortal body failing, God wants to save our souls from death.

John 16-33: "I have told you these things so that you may have peace. In this world, you will have trouble. But take heart! I have overcome the world" Keeping my eyes on Jesus when going through hard times leads my soul in a heavenly direction.

Philippians 4:6-7: "Do not be anxious about anything, but in everything, by prayer and petition, with understanding present your requests to God. And the peace of God, which transcends all understanding, will guard your hearts and minds in Christ Jesus." Even at troubled times, ask God to help you. God will give you peace beyond anything this world can provide you.

Philippians 4:8-9: "Finally brothers, whatever is true, whatever is noble, whatever is right, whatever is pure, whatever is lovely, whatever is admirable--if anything is excellent or praiseworthy--think about such things. Whatever you have learned or received or heard from Me--put into practice. And the God of peace will be with you."

In this appeal, Paul is asking us to think positive thoughts. If we do, God's peace that passes all understanding will stay inside you. Regardless of the world around you, God's peace will give you the strength to carry on.

Regardless of the circumstances, I pray people hurting are drawn to God, knowing there is comfort in His arms. I am in awe of how people are reaching out and helping others. I pray some good will come out of all the sickness that surrounds our world. I pray that God will heal our nation!

CHAPTER 22

Limitations

We can limit the power of God by the way we live. We can define the power of God by what we want. We can limit the power of God by not reading the Bible. When we go back to our old ways, we can limit God's ability to make us stronger.

How often do we limit the power of God because we are judgmental? How often do we determine the power of God because we won't let go? Even in our personal lives, we can limit God's power by making decisions on our own.

We study the Old Testament because we don't want history to repeat itself. The Israelites spent forty years in a wilderness because of their rebellion. Because of their disobedience, they became governed by people they should have managed. God wanted them to become more faithful. They were a ten-day journey from the promised land. They would lack the discipline, and they never got there.

We limit the power of God because of our rebellion. God can't help us if we continue making mistakes that hurt us in the past. We restrict the authority God has to change our lives. We end up giving up; we end up in worse conditions than before we met Jesus. Mending our lives take time; are we willing to be patient? Are we willing to work on some of our weaknesses?

Psalm 90:4: "For a thousand years in your sight are like a day that has just gone by, or like a watch in the night." When we get discouraged, and it seems like our life is going nowhere. Reading the verse above, I realize, time means nothing to God. A thousand years is like a day to God. Don't limit the power of God and His ability to see into your future. Verse 8: "You have set our iniquities before your secret sins in the light of Your presence." God knows everything about us. Don't be afraid to come to Him and ask Him for help. We limit God's power because we don't ask Him to help us!

In the book of Luke, we read about Zechariah. He was a priest who served God. According to custom, He would go into the temple and burn incense. "Then an angel from the Lord appeared to him, standing at the right side of the altar of incense,(luke 1:11.)" Verse 13; The angel told him not to be afraid, and his wife would bear a child. Even people who know God can doubt His power to achieve what seems impossible. We know Elizabeth would get pregnant, and that child was John the Baptist.

Luke 1:13: "But the angel said to him: 'Do not be afraid, Zechariah: your prayer has been heard.' Your wife Elizabeth will bear you a son, and you are to give him the name John." John, in different languages, means, "the Lord is gracious," and Jesus translated, "The Lord saves." God sent John into the world to pave the way for Jesus to come. Jesus came to save the world!

The angel goes on in verse 15 by saying, "For he will be great in the sight of the Lord. He is never to take wine or other fermented drink, and he will be filled with the Holy Spirit even from birth." For the first time, the Holy Spirit was mentioned in the New Testament. Luke also wrote the Book of Acts; he knew from experience how the Holy Spirit could change his life. Throughout the Bible, people filled with the Holy Spirit; would do things that seem impossible.

2 Corinthians 12:7: "To keep me from becoming conceited because of these surpassing revelations, there was given to me a thorn in my

flesh, a messenger from Satan, to torment me." Paul was brilliant, but something happened to him, and it kept him from getting conceited. At times we can think we have all the answers, but life has a way of making us humble. Verse 8: "Three times I pleaded with the Lord to take it away from me."

Maybe God was limiting Paul's ability to feel secure? Perhaps we limit God's ability to help us when we try doing things on our own? Verse 9a: "But He(God) said to me, 'My grace is sufficient for you, for my power is made perfect in weakness.'" Maybe Paul got tired of fighting on his own and finally let God help him? Do we need to struggle before we ask God to help us?

Verse 9b: "Therefore, I will boast all the more gladly about my weaknesses so that Christ's power may rest on me. Verse 10, Paul begins to learn what God is telling him; 'That is why, for Christ's sake. I delight in weaknesses, in insults, in hardships, in persecutions, in difficulties. For when I am weak, then I am strong."

We limit God's power by trying to do things on our own. When I quit fighting and admit I am weak, then God can help me to be healthy. I don't know what was going through Paul's mind, but just like Paul, I am learning not to limit God's power. When I try to handle things on my own, I often fail. If I admit; I am weak, then God has the potential to make me secure!

Learning To Resist Temptation

Genesis 3:1: "Now the serpent was more crafty than any animals the LORD God had made. He said to the woman, 'Did God say,' You must not eat from any tree in the garden?" Satan used doubt so he could get into Eve's head. After I read this scripture, I think to myself, how often I fail, and Satan comes in and tries to destroy the progress I have made. God doesn't want us to dwell on failure; He knows we will fail!

I have learned resisting Satan can truly make us more reliable, but at times I am still weak and give in. I am so thankful I have a God who still loves me and accepts me when I fall short of His glory. God doesn't punish or condemn us; the Holy Spirit shows me how my weaknesses hurt me.

I had to ask myself, what is the reward for giving in to temptation? Is the reward worth the risks we are taking? When it comes to watching the opposite sex or eating a sweet when we aren't hungry, is the reward worth the trouble we are making?

Many of our instincts have only given us pleasure for the moment. Many of us would look for love in all the wrong places. We live in a world that says happiness is the product of getting the things we want. Many of us are compulsive and want immediate satisfaction. Often going to the refrigerator or even going out and shopping; Do we do these things to avoid our inner self? Does looking for love in all the wrong places help you to feel more secure? After becoming a Christian, I began to look at all these areas in my life. When the Holy Spirit shows me what I need to change, I know dwelling on these moments only makes me weaker. I started asking myself, why do I do these things?

If you have a compulsive personality, it's hard to be strong in weak areas. Learning to deal with ourselves takes time and patience. It isn't always easy to be spiritual. Many times we measure spiritual growth by gradually changing. Having God's Spirit inside you gives us strength, but it doesn't mean I will always use His Spirit to avoid temptation. God knows what we will do before we do it, and He also knows how hard we try. I measure growth not by counting the times when I have failed but by my progress.

Philippians 1:9-11: "And this is my prayer; that your love may abound more and more in knowledge and depth of insight so that you may be able to discern what is best and may be pure and blameless until the day of Christ filled with the fruits of righteousness that comes through Jesus Christ--to the glory and praise of God." God's word is speaking out to us in this prayer. Knowledge and insight will help us realize just how much God loves us and how His righteousness can help. Discernment: This means learning what is right and wrong.

Romans 7:7: "What shall we say, then? Is the law sin? Certainly not! Indeed I would not have known what sin was except through the law." Because we have studied the law and the Ten Commandments, we understand how sin can affect us. Exploring the Old Testament, I begin to understand how rebellion against the rule caused the Israelites problems. Paul used coveting as an example. We wouldn't have known about coveting and how it affects how we live unless God gave us the Ten Commandments.

Verse 13: "Did that which is good, then, become death to me. By no means! But in order for sin might be recognized as sin, it produced death in me through what was good, so that through the Commandments sin might become utterly sinful." If we followed the commands of God, think about all the pain and heartache we could have avoided. When we sin, we are truly hurting ourselves. I ask myself, "Did that which was good, then, become death to me?"

Verse 14-15: "We know the law is spiritual, but I am unspiritual, sold to sin. I do not understand what I do. For what I do I do not do, but what I hate I do." Here it seems Paul is having problems doing the right thing. Instead of doing the right thing, he does the opposite. When Paul talks about being unspiritual, Paul talks about rebellion. He talks about the struggle; we sin, but we don't want to sin.

Verse 20: "Now if I do what I do not want to do, it no longer is I that do it, but it is a sin living in me that does it." It's only because of God's Spirit living in us that we have any control over sin. Sometimes we are unable to defend ourselves, and we give in to sin. Being human, we all have a sinful nature.

He continues in verses 24-25a by saying: "What a wretched man I am! Who will rescue me from this body of death? Thanks be to God--through Jesus Christ, our Lord!" Paul once again is talking about the internal struggle that we go through. We should thank God for any of the power we have to stop sinning. Jesus Christ gave you victory over sin. Paul ends by saying in verse 25b: "So then, I myself in my mind am a slave to God's law, but in a sinful nature a slave to the law of sin." We want to obey God's laws, but being human, sin is still in our bodies.

Romans 8:1-2: "Therefore, there is no condemnation for those who are in Christ Jesus, because through Christ Jesus the law of life set me free from the law of sin and death." I'm so thankful I am not under law and condemnation, but Christ Jesus' grace and mercy. I have lived through the Spirit, and the Spirit gives me strength that leads to victory.

I can't lift myself by my bootstraps; the harder I try will lead to failure. It's the Spirit inside me who gives me any power. When I fail, all I can do is pray, and I ask God for His forgiveness.

2 Corinthians 10:3-5: "For though we live in the world, we do not rage war as the world does. The weapons we fight with are not weapons of the world. On the contrary, they have divine power to demolish arguments that set up against the knowledge of God, and take captive every thought to make it obedient to Christ."

I think about how I feel, "The devil made me do it or "I'm only human." God has given us power over Satan, claiming I am human and weak are thoughts that I can change. My favorite, "I'm not good enough." The Spirit inside me has the divine power to change those thoughts.

Resisting those thoughts can help, but I need to address those thoughts when they happen. We can't always control our thinking, but we need to stop, don't dwell on those thoughts. Take those thoughts and make them obedient to Christ.

Ephesians 6:10-11: "Finally be strong in the Lord and His mighty power. Put on the full armor of God so you can take a stand against the devil's schemes." Reading scripture and staying grounded will lead to thinking less about the world and focusing on God. If I don't do the things that keep us grounded, we can lose all the control God has given us. At times ask yourself, is the reward worth the risks I take? Has the world become more important than God?

Ephesians 6:12-15: "For our struggle is not against flesh and blood, but against the rulers, against the authorities, against the powers of this world and the spiritual forces of evil in the heavenly realms. Therefore put on the full armor of God, so that when the day of evil comes, you may be able to stand your ground, and after you have done everything, to stand."

Satan does exist, and his mission is to keep us weak. If we don't plant our feet on solid ground, we can't grow spiritually. The spiritual life is a journey. We might take three steps forward; then, we fail; giving up isn't an option. Putting on the whole armor of God means reading my Bible, going to church, not avoiding people who can help me. Don't allow Satan to plant doubts; you are making progress. The spiritual life isn't about being perfect or having all the answers; it's about our progress!

Loneliness

The one thing many of us felt was loneliness. We know the feeling of being abandoned. Many of us looked at the mirror and didn't like what we see. Toward the end, many got to the point of desperation and tried killing themselves. We know the feeling of failure when life didn't work out, the sense of how we beat ourselves up, thinking we failed again!

Then we have the modern man and woman. They have good jobs, can buy anything they want, people look up to them, and continually have goals they can accomplish. Their family loves them, and they have friends and parties. They live lives, not worrying about tomorrow. This is the world's idea of success.

Exodus 6:10-12: "Then the Lord said to Moses, 'Go, tell Pharoah King of Egypt to let the Israelites go out of his country.' But Moses said to the LORD, 'If the Israelites will not listen to me, why would Pharoah listen to me since I speak with faltering lips?'" God helped him to overcome his loneliness. I'm sure he had to feel lonely, having to face Pharoah and all his subjects.

Look at the life of Jeremiah; He was one of God's prophets. Jeremiah was poor; people would avoid him, being rejected by his family, he knew the feeling of isolation. He knew how God had an answer but had to watch his nation crumble before his eyes. God considered this man to be successful, even after being put into exile, would continue to prophesy!

Even when the Holy Spirit calls us to say or do something, loneliness can be an excuse, and we do nothing. If the Holy Spirit convicts us to do something, this is God's way of helping us.

God can use loneliness to draw us close to Him. At times like this, God is building our character. He wants us to see areas that are weak and help those areas to grow stronger. Meditating He gives us solutions, things we can do so we won't feel so lonely.

1 Kings 19:13: "And the word of the LORD appeared to him, 'What are you doing here, Elijah?' He replied, " I have been very zealous for the LORD God Almighty.' The Israelites have rejected your covenant, broken down Your altars, and put Your prophets to death with the sword, I am the only one left, and they are trying to kill me too."

Elijah watched the King's court and the priesthood turn corrupt. Because he felt threatened, he forgot about the people who remained faithful to God. Lonely and discouraged, he ran to Mount Horeb. God gave him high strength to walk the two hundred miles to reach Mount Horeb.

Mt Horeb is the sacred place Moses went years ago, and God gave Moses the laws to give the Israelites. Just like Moses did centuries ago, Elijah fasted for forty days and nights.

1 Kings 19:11: "The LORD said, 'Go to the mountain in the presence of the LORD, for the LORD is about to pass by.'" Verse 13-15: We read about an earthquake and fire coming, how Elijah pulled his cloak over his eyes and how God talked to him in a gentle voice. God told him to go back and appoint certain Kings in certain areas. Verse

18; There were 7,000 who hadn't bowed down to Baal. Bowing down to Baal, people were worshiping an object that wasn't God. Even though Elijah was lonely and filled with fear, he still had work to do.

Elijah was a loner, but he paid the price for his isolation. When our world is in turmoil, sit back and meditate on God's word, and in a gentle voice, He will answer you. Don't sit around feeling lonely and filled with self-pity; take your concerns to God, and He will give you what you need. Being a Spirit-filled Christian, it might seem like you are alone, but God's spirit is inside you; you are not alone!

A big part of not feeling lonely is finding friends that you can call. Get involved at church. If you are genuinely searching, God will open doors. Use the resources that God will lay at your feet. The hardest part of the journey is taking the first step forward.

David wrote many of the Psalms; He wrote many of them when he felt lonely and depressed. When I feel alone, and my world feels torn apart, I read some of those Psalms. Reading the Psalms, I invite God to be a part of my spirit.

Proverbs 18:24: "A man of many companions may come to ruin, but there is a friend who sticks closer than a brother." Finding Jesus, I have learned the value of real friendship. Many times I am a phone call away from help. If I am genuinely seeking to do the will of God, doors will open.

I spent many years in the wilderness of my own making. There are good people out there who pay a small lifetime all alone. You look for love in all the wrong places; you never lose the feeling of being alone. Jesus can open doors that will take you to another location. Don't limit God's ability to open doors!

Isaiah 58:6: "Is not this the kind of fasting I have chosen; to loose the chains of injustice and untie the cords of the yoke, to set the oppressed free and break every yoke?" Can God break the yoke of loneliness! How can Jesus set the oppressed free?

Verse 7: "Is it not to share your food with the hungry and to provide the poor wanderer with shelter--when you see the naked, to clothe him and not to turn away from your own flesh and blood?" One way to set the oppressed free is by helping someone who needs help!

Verse 8:Then your light will break forth like the dawn, and your healing will quickly appear; then your righteousness will go before you, and the glory of the LORD will be your rear guard." In verse 6, God is telling us to fast, but personal fast is only helping us. He wants our service to go beyond ourselves. Instead of feeling lonely, we need to use some action.

Verse 9-10: "Then you will call, and the LORD will answer; you will cry for help, and He will say. Here I am. If you do away with the yoke of oppression, with the pointing finger and malicious talk, and if you spend yourselves on behalf of the hungry and satisfy the needs of the oppressed, then your light will rise in the darkness, and your night will become like the noonday."

God is giving us the key to ending our oppression. By helping others, your light will shine in the darkness. Don't sit around talking about your loneliness; reach out and help someone. Find a good church, go to Bible studies, talk to your Pastor about the problems you are having. Call a friend!

Hebrews 12:1-2: "Therefore, since we are surrounded by a great cloud of witnesses, let us throw off everything that hinders and the sin that so easily entangles, and let us run with perseverance the race marked out for us. Let us fix our eyes on Jesus, the Author and Perfector of our faith, Who for the joy set before Him endured the cross, scouring His shame. and sat down at the right hand of the throne of God."

Moses, Elijah, and David are some of the high clouds of witnesses. They had to face everything that we might be going through, facing these obstacles and their perseverance made them more durable. Jeremiah faced conditions many of us will never experience but continued to prophesy till he died. Jesus scorned the shame, and His death, knowing the joy we would feel!

Hebrews 13:5-7: "Keep your eyes free from the love of money and be content with what you have because God has said, 'Never will I leave you; never will I forsake you.' So say with confidence, 'The Lord is my helper; I will not be afraid, What can man do to me?'" Remember your leaders, who spoke the word of God to you. Consider the outcome of their way of life and imitate their faith. Jesus Christ is the same yesterday and today and forever."

Not being content with what God has given me can lead to loneliness. Living in the past can create a deep hole for us. We can get lonely and depressed by not living one day at a time. These are things I often look at when I feel all alone. Putting our trust in Jesus can help us crawl out of the hole that can only get deeper!

1 Peter 5:6-7: "Humble yourselves, therefore, under God's mighty hand, that He might lift you up in due time. Cast all your anxiety on Him because He cares for you." When we are lonely and filled with anxiety, we can pray. Regardless of how far you have fallen, still call on Him for help. When we call on Him for help, He can draw us closer to Him.

Verses 10-11: "And the God of all grace, Who called you to His eternal glory in Christ, after you have suffered a little while, will Himself restore you and make you strong, firm and steadfast. To Him, be the power forever and ever. Amen."

God doesn't want us to face our problems alone. That's why He gave us the Holy Spirit, and He even puts people on our path who can help us. Thinking we can handle life on our own is the devil's way of keeping us from doing what we need to do. When the Holy Spirit tells us to call someone, go somewhere, we need to follow. God is giving us a door, but I need to hear His calling and open the door!

Psalm 32

People have torn down relationships with family and friends; we are worn down by guilt and in need of forgiveness. Many souls are in bondage because of their inability to let go of the past. Guilt keeps us isolated, unable to move forward!

In Psalm 32, David is going to God and asking Him for forgiveness. He had sinned against Bathsheba and Uriah, and he was asking God to forgive his transgressions. David knew what he did was wrong. David knew the only person that could relieve his guilty conscience was God.

Exodus 34:7a: "The Lord, the Lord, the compassionate and gracious God. slow to anger, abounding in love and faithfulness, maintaining love to thousands, and forgiving wickedness, rebellion, and sin." God revealed himself to Moses and in future generations to David, then in more significant fashion to the world by sending down His only begotten Son, our Lord, and Savior Jesus Christ.

He goes on in verse 7b: telling us, He doesn't leave the guilty unpunished. Many generations are affected by people who don't seek forgiveness. You look at alcoholism and child abuse; second and third generations can influence(affect) their children by how they were mistreated in the past. The cycle stops with you and me. The process can stop when we make Jesus our Lord and Savior! We have to be sorry for the sins we committed; only Jesus has the power to forgive us of those sins!

Psalms 32:1: "Blessed is he whose transgressions are forgiven, whose sins are covered." David knew only God could forgive his transgressions. Because we have faith that Jesus died on the cross and we are genuinely sorry for the way we treated others and the sins we committed, we too can receive forgiveness.

Psalm 32:2: "Blessed is the man whose sin the Lord does not count against him and in whose spirit is no deceit." David knew he could go to God and receive forgiveness. David worshiped the same God we worship, which shows us love, compassion, and forgiveness.

Psalm 32:4: "For day and night, your hand was heavy upon me; my strength was sapped as in the heat of summer." What good does quilt accomplish? Feeling guilty lays a heavy hand upon our spirit, and we can't move forward. If God forgives us, feeling guilty is a punishment we put on ourselves. If I continue exploring guilty, maybe our conscience is saying I need to make an amend? Meditating the Holy Spirit always gives me a course of action that I can follow.

Psalm 32:5: "Then I acknowledged my sin to you and did not cover up my iniquity. I said, 'I will confess my transgressions to the Lord'--and You will forgive the guilt of my sin." How long must we wait before we go to Jesus asking for our forgiveness? There isn't a reward for holding on to the quilt?

We can hold on to guilt for a lifetime. After receiving absolution, there isn't any reward for feeling guilty. I spent a short lifetime mulling over guilt, unable to move forward. When things would go wrong in my life, I would always feel guilty. When I say or do something I regret, this is God's way of showing me I am human. The world doesn't always see things my way. I am starting to do the right things, and God gives me the approval I need.

Psalm 32: 6: "Therefore let everyone who is godly pray to You while You may be found; surely when the mighty waters rise, they will not reach him." I no longer wait days before going to God for forgiveness. When I am wrong, I go to God, asking for His forgiveness. Then, before the mighty waters come(quilt), I can make the changes necessary to get back into God's graces(repentance.)

Psalm 32:7: "You are my hiding place; You will protect me from trouble and surround me with songs of deliverance." For those who found Jesus, God has become our hiding place. He protects us when we try doing what is right. He surrounds us with His comfort and His love.

Verses 8: He will instruct you and teach you in the way you should go; I will counsel you and watch over you." God knows our hearts, and if we are sincere, He will guide us in the right direction. Verse 9: He compares some people to a horse or a mule with no understanding and continues to sin. He wants us to be sincere and know why we need forgiveness. We can't go to Him after we willingly keep sinning and want His mercy.

We can't undo our past and some of the things we did. But with God's guidance, we can change. I learned three things from Psalm 32: Confession, repentance, and forgiveness. God always responds to us when we confess our sins. Repentance means I am genuinely sorry for the crimes I committed; I began to change with God's guidance. I learned God has the power to forgive, and when we continue feeling quilt, we only punish ourselves!

Verses 10-11: "Many are the woes of the wicked, but the Lord's unfailing love surrounds the man who trusts in Him. Rejoice in the Lord and be glad, you righteous; sing, all you who are upright in heart."

The spiritual life is a journey, there are times when we move forward, but then we might fail and go back to our old ways. This process of transformation takes time and patience. God knows if we are doing the best we can do and is quick to forgive us. Knowing what needs attention is a gift when we fall short of our expectations; We know what needs our attention.

Like so many in the world today, I fought depression my entire life. Depression only keeps our soul in bondage; Guilt is a way of holding on to yesterday. God will answer your prayers by giving you His forgiveness. His forgiveness gives us the ability to let go of the past and the mistakes we have made. If we are genuinely sorry for those sins, you have been forgiven!

Prayer

We live in a world of our making; many of humanity's choices aren't the choices God would make. We can live and die by the choices we make. In my Christian life, change can lead to victory.

DO YOU KNOW THE TRUTH?

We know the effects of overeating and how working too hard can lead to an early death, but do people listen and try changing their ways. We hear people say, "It wasn't his time to die." God knows everything, and He knows when we will die. He never said we wouldn't get sick, that this world wouldn't be challenging. Life has turning points, but do we learn our lessons and change our ways?

When I started reading the Book of Proverbs, God gave me a picture of my life. Solomon wrote this book centuries ago, but the cause and effects of how we live have never changed. Knowledge is good, but do we take that knowledge and learn? Do we learn our lessons or continue making the same mistakes? God can show us the right way to live; does that mean we won't have any hardships?

Proverbs 1:7: "The fear of the Lord is the beginning of knowledge; fools despise wisdom and instruction." We know what is harmful, but do we stop? The fear of God means being in awe of His power. After I felt the Holy Spirit fill me, I knew God's Spirit could change our soul and life altogether. Does learning and doing this knowledge lead to wisdom?

Reading the Book of Proverbs, I saw myself through God's eyes for the first time. I learned the exact nature of my wrongs and how it has affected my life in many ways. Proverbs gave me knowledge, acting, and changing the behavior would lead to wisdom.

I went to Catholic school; being a depressed child, I never knew prayer's benefits until I was older. I remember going home, and my house was empty. My first wife took my son and would file for divorce. I remember kneeling and asking God to help me. I haven't had any alcohol or street drugs since that night. We never know how God will answer our prayers. Life closed one door, but God gave me what I needed!

Romans 8:28: "And we know for those who love God all things work together for good for those who are called according to His purpose." I didn't understand that verse until I found Jesus. I am learning that God will make some good come out of any bad situation we might be facing. I have learned in my personal experience; there are two parts to prayer;

asking and meditation. Meditation: the art of listening to what the Holy Spirit is trying to tell me.

The key to knowing how God can answer my prayers is by learning what I need. Instead of praying for what I want, I ask God to give me what I need. I know God answers our wants when we are ready. I wouldn't be the person I am today if God gave me everything I wanted. Just because we are Christians doesn't make us immune to the world and all its problems. Praying to God keeps our lives moving in the right direction. Through prayer, I could rise above any of the circumstances I was facing.

One of my friends in the Bible study passed away; I asked God to help his family recover from their loss. My friend at work might have cancer; I ask God to heal Him. I haven't talked to my son in over three months. I was praying to God that somehow He could reach my son. I am asking God to give me the strength and the understanding to know; I am doing the right thing by letting go.

When you have done all you can do, said all you can say, my only choice is to pray. All I can do is ask, but I know God answers prayer at His time!

My wife grew up in an abusive environment. She was saved and baptized at an early age. God gave her the strength to survive. God uses her power to help people. God answered her prayers by giving her the courage to keep moving forward. When she was old enough, God gave her the courage to move and her willingness to heal. My wife wasn't a victim but a survivor!

We did a study on prayer; the author said there are four parts to our prayers. One is adoration, praising God for being in our lives. Through prayer, we show Him deep love and give Him our respect. Honor, raising Him above any pain and suffering we may be facing.

God is greater than he that is in the world. He is the devil who tries to tell us that prayer doesn't work at trying times in our lives. He is the sickness that can destroy us. He is the anger and unforgiveness we can carry around. God is greater than the abusive situations we are facing.

Prayer can give us the strength to survive. Prayer(asking) and meditation(listening) can help us make the right decisions. In many cases, accepting Jesus as our Lord and Savior is the answer to our prayers.

The second part of why we pray is a confession, confessing to God the sins we committed and asking Him for His forgiveness. We can admit our doubts, any shortcomings we may have had; God always hears our prayers. Even while feeling all alone, prayers to God can give us comfort. Listening(meditation) provides us with a path that we can follow.

The third reason we pray is thanksgiving; we are thanking God for being in our lives. When things are good or bad, we thank Him for being a part of our lives. We thank Him for the opportunity to make Him a part of everything going on in our personal lives.

He spoke about supplication as being the fourth; this means praying to God with intensity and perseverance. My mom prayed for me for many years while I was going through some bad times. She never saw the result of those prayers, but she never quit praying. When the time came, God gave her the courage to let go!

He also mentioned intercession(petition); that is what I am doing this morning, praying God can help my loved ones see the light. What else can I do? The only power I have is in God's hands, not mine!

Psalms 145:1-2: "I will exalt You, my God and King; I will praise your name forever and ever. Every day I will praise You and extol Your name forever and ever." This psalm starts with David giving God the adoration and respect that only God deserves.

Psalms 51:1-2: "Have mercy on me, O God, according to Your unfailing love; according to Your great compassion blot out my transgressions. Wash away all my iniquity and cleanse me from my sin." David knew sleeping with Bathsheba was the wrong thing to do and then sending her husband into war, knowing he would die. Confession: David was asking God for His forgiveness.

Psalm 61:1-3: "Hear my cry, O God; listen to my prayer. From the ends of the earth, I call to you; I call as my heart grows faint; lead me to the rock that is higher than I. For you have been my refuge, a strong tower against the foe." David knew seeking God's council would save him from his enemies. David would pray before making any significant decisions. When times seemed out of control, David would pray!

Matthew 26:42: "He went away a second time and prayed, 'My Father, if it is not possible for this cup to be taken away unless I drink it, may your will be done.'" Even at the darkest hour in the Garden of Gethsemane, Jesus would pray to His Father in heaven. He was praying for the strength to do His Father's will. Even praying for our wants to be answered; we try ending those prayers by saying, "Your will be done!"

God would love to answer many of our prayers. When they involve others, God gives everyone a choice to make their own decisions. Those decisions aren't the ones God wants them to make, but He allows them to happen.

Luke 6:12-13a: "One of those days, Jesus went out to the mountainside to pray, and spent the night praying to God. When morning came, He called His disciples to Him and chose twelve of them, whom He designated apostles." Even Jesus would pray before making any significant decisions. Jesus always set an example for us to follow.

Luke 11: 1-4: "One day Jesus was praying in a certain place. When He was finished, one of His disciples said to Him, 'Lord, teach us how to pray, just as John taught his disciples.' He said to them, "Father, hallowed be thy name." Here they(we) are praising God by addressing Him as their(our) heavenly Father. Hallowed be thy name, they(we) acknowledge Him as sacred and holy by placing His name above all names. He will give us His full attention whenever we call on God, "your kingdom come."

Verse 3: "Give us Your daily bread." We begin by asking God to give us the inspiration and encouragement to face our day. We are asking God to provide us with what we need. His joy inside our heart is the strength to get through the day if we need His comfort, the knowledge that He is there, and listening. We ask for strength and wisdom, the ability to handle any situation that might cross our path.

"Forgive us of our sins, for we also forgive everyone who sins against us." If we have sinned(confession) asking Him to forgive any sins we committed. If someone has sinned against us having the same forgiveness that God has always shown me. "And lead us not into temptation." We ask God to help us avoid temptation. Regardless of how people act, we still treat them with love!

In the Lord's prayer, we are asking God to give us what we need. God often reminds me of when I pray; prayer is not a substitute for being someone's answer to their prayers. Sometimes we are God's answer when people pray for His help!

CHAPTER 23

Who's Right, Who's Wrong?

I'm not proud that I am working on my third marriage, but I am. Looking back at my other unions, I see just how much I needed to learn about love. Finding Jesus has been a key that has kept my third marriage together. I wish I could say things are running smoothly, but we still have some disagreements. I remember one, in particular; this argument taught me a lesson.

I am up north, alone again; my wife and I disagreed. When we fight, I forget what started the fight, and then it becomes a question: who's right and who's wrong? This time, I will not be the one who ends the argument that is usually mistake number one. Then I will refuse to call, which is mistake number two. Then it becomes a question of hurt pride, and that is mistake number three!

The difference in this marriage is how God can intercede despite our differences. Mistake number four is thinking she might call. After a couple of days when I don't call, I decide to see my father-in-law, who lives fifty miles away.

Going into his house, I realize he isn't feeling good. He needed medicine, and my wife knew the name of the medicine he needs. Jesus helped me to do the right thing, and I called her. One week later, my father-in-law passed away. Can you imagine the guilt I would feel if I didn't call? She would have to deal with her dad's death and my selfishness.

It doesn't matter to God, who is right, and who is wrong. What matters is doing the right thing in the eyes of God. I know the dysfunction my wife had to deal with when she was growing up. Dealing with dysfunction made her a healthy person. It isn't me that will change her; that is something only God has the power to do. Since that day, I am learning the role I play in this marriage. There are times when I could teach her a better way of doing things, but I can't force that change to happen. It has to be on her terms and God's timing.

St. Francis of Assisi was an Italian Catholic friar. He wrote a prayer that has always stayed with me since I got sober years ago. Francis's life had emotional wringers, just like mine. He wrote a prayer that he tried to aspire to throughout his life. When I read this prayer, I see how God wants me to live my life. Whenever I read this prayer, it teaches me how to live a spiritual experience.

"Lord, make me a channel of thy peace--that where there is hatred, I may bring love--that where it is wrong, I may bring the spirit of forgiveness--that where there is discord, I may bring harmony--where there is an error, I may bring truth--where there is doubt, I may bring faith--where there is despair, I bring hope--that where there are shadows, I may bring light--that where there is sadness, I may bring joy. Lord, grant that I may seek rather to comfort than to be comforted--to understand than to be understood--to love than to be loved. For it is by self-forgetting that one finds. It is by forgiving one is forgiven. It is by dying that one awakens to eternal life. Amen"

Practicing this prayer in all my affairs leads me to be one with God's heart and soul. Reading this prayer even at times when I am hurting will lead my soul to eternal life. Francis of Assisi is a person trying to be selfless. He lived in a spiritual experience.

Before meeting Jesus, I thought how I act on the outside is different than how I should perform at home. After meeting Jesus, I thought, why shouldn't I serve at home the way I do in the outside world? Maybe that could show my wife how God is changing me?

After her father passed away, I started to look at our marriage differently. I began to look at my roles in the union and what God could change. I began to listen to what she was trying to tell me and started making boundaries that would keep us from arguing. When she was stubborn, I would be forgiving. Then God started showing me the good things that were in her and why I got married. We went through two significant deaths. Instead of those deaths pulling us apart, we became closer.

Ephesians 5:25-28: "Husbands love your wives, just as Christ loved the church and gave Himself up to her to make her holy, cleansing her by the washing with water through the word, and to present her to Himself as a radiant church, without stain or wrinkle or any blemish, but holy and blameless. In the same way, husbands ought to love their wives as their bodies. He who loves his wife loves himself." Our wives are an extension of ourselves. How do we love our wives? 1. By thinking about them first and what can make them happy. 2. By treating them with kindness and with love.

God doesn't want our marriages to fail. He wants to heal them and make them stronger. I try making decisions that benefit both of us. I have learned to put my pride aside and do things right in God's eyes. God is showing me the battle is inside me, not in changing my wife. All marriages go through ups and downs, but because we found God together, I can see the answers that will keep us together!

CHAPTER 24

Time To Change

We know the story about David and Bathsheba. David committed a sin, slept with her, and then sent her husband into a war zone, knowing her husband would die. The Lord sent Nathan to confront David. David heard a story about how a rich man took the cow of a poor man and prepared dinner for his guest.

2 Samuel 12:5-6: "David burned with anger against the man and said to Nathan, 'As surely as the Lord lives, the man who does this deserves to die!' He must pay for the lamb four times because he did such a thing and had no pity. Then Nathan said to David, 'You are the man!'" David made a sentence on himself; David and Bathsheba lost four sons at birth. The fifth son was Solomon, and he became King of Israel.

Solomon wrote the Book of Proverbs; He was one of the wisest kings of Israel. People came from all over to hear his wisdom. Solomon wrote his knowledge in the Book of Proverbs. Much of what we know as common sense--he wrote in Proverbs.

As Solomon got older, he looked at his life and realized it all was meaningless. The only thing that had any meaning was his relationship with God. Pleasure, oppression, toil, and advancement all these things amounted to nothing. Have you ever been at a time in your life and ask yourself; Is everything I do have any meaning? After all his striving to achieve all his pride in what he had done, it all felt meaningless.

Maybe you are sick and tired of living or going through a divorce; perhaps you feel lonely and depressed. You are old and tired, and all your effort to achieve has been taken away. The realization that the heart attack I was going through could kill me, and I couldn't do anything to stop it! At times like these, we can feel hopeless. All the things we put importance on mean nothing. In a moment, we can lose everything!

I went through an operation years ago; my arm ended up with an infection. At first, I thought, what good is my life without using an arm, living seemed meaningless, and I got angry and resentful. God still gave me hope, and I went to therapy three times a week for over a year. I got the feeling back into my arm, and I could do things. It was God's Spirit inside me that gave me hope. When tragic things happen in our lives, we tend to look at our life differently.

I was on the verge of going through another divorce; I felt lost; knowing all I had done wasn't enough. Shortly afterward, I found Jesus. He gave me a way of life that would lead my life in a better direction. As I get older, I realize how my life would be meaningless without Jesus and the Holy Spirit.

Reading Ecclesiastes chapter three, I began to realize there is a time for everything. Verses 1 to 8 in Ecclesiastes: I see how it was a time to let Jesus in and a time to change. Maybe this was a time for Solomon to see his life and give us a message that will bring meaning and hope into your life? Solomon had all the riches this world could offer him, but reflecting on all the things he had, it all felt meaningless to him. The only thing that had any meaning was God!

When addiction controlled my life, I remember coming home, and it was empty. My wife had taken my son, and a divorce notice was on a table. I remember getting on my knees and asking God to help me; I haven't had a drink of alcohol or any street drugs since that night.

I have been sober by the grace of God for over forty years. AA (alcoholics anonymous) showed me three alternatives: recovery, more insanity, or death. Making Jesus my Lord and Savior was another moment in my life, and I was at the crossroads of life once again. Once again, I looked at those three options: change, running, losing everything once again!

Ecclesiastes 3:1: "There is a time for everything and a season for every activity under heaven." God has a plan for everyone. I had to get to the point when I didn't have any more answers. I was genuinely sick of losing and having to start over. I had to put my faith in someone other than myself. This season would lead to having activity under heaven. Jesus gave me a way to live my life. Doing things His way would lead to eternal freedom.

Verse 2: "A time to be born and a time to die, a time to plant and a time to uproot." Why does God mention being born and dying in the same verse? Then a time to plant and uproot? After meeting Jesus, my old life and thinking began to disappear. Finding Jesus, filled with the Holy Spirit, I was born again. Striving to do His will in all my affairs, I could plant seeds that helped me uproot and grow.

Verse 3: "A time to kill and a time to heal, a time to tear down and a time to build." A time to kill is a strong word used by God to make us realize the nature of how we use to live. I had to tear down the walls of prejudice that I had been feeling for many years. Through faith that Jesus lived and died for me, those walls started to come down. Because Jesus died and made atonement for the sins we committed, I could receive God's forgiveness. I could be born again and start over.

Verse 4: "A time to weep and a time to laugh, a time to mourn and a time to dance." Weeping and remorse would make me regret the past and the harm I caused others. Because I was sorry for the sins I committed in the past(repentance), I started changing into a different person. My world filled with remorse, and weeping took a gradual turn, and I learned how to laugh. I started living the way Jesus wanted me to live; instead of sorrow, my spirit learned to dance!

Verse 5: "A time to scatter stones and a time to gather them, a time to embrace and a time to refrain." My life was like stones scattered all over the place. My mind was like a chameleon changing colors. I had to learn how to embrace God and learning to refrain from doing things the old way.

Verse 6: "A time to search and a time to give up a time to keep and a time to throw away." I had to learn how to reach out to God and ask Him to help me. I had to surrender to God everything that was part of me. Jesus showed me what was good inside me that I could keep. The anger and hurt, the past, and what I thought was happiness; these things I had to throw away.

Verse 7: "A time to tear and a time to mend, a time to be silent and a time to speak." Tearing down my walls, I begin to mend. Jesus taught me how to live, when to talk or when to be silent. God gave me the courage to change myself. The ability to see what I could change and when to let go!

Verse 8: "A time to love and a time to hate, a time for war and a time for peace." God taught me to love myself and to share that love with others. I learned the meaning of hating some of the things in the outside world. I could war against the injustice and the darkness that exists in the world around me. Leaning on Him, He gave me peace beyond my understanding.

Reading the Bible, I learned how I should live. Striving to live the way He taught me, the Holy Spirit filled my spirit. I started fighting my battles one day at a time. God gave me the answers that would lead to peace and healing. I learned to let go of the past and being grateful for the people and the life He has given me. Without Jesus in my life, my life would be meaningless!

DO YOU KNOW THE TRUTH?

I have been a Christian for over ten years; whenever I feel lost or going through mental pain, I realize that it would all be meaningless(life) without Jesus in my life!

CHAPTER 25

To the Oppressed

The definition of oppressed: The feeling of being heavily burdened mentally or physically. Trouble, adverse conditions, relationships, all these things can keep you oppressed.

You are the ones who wander and stay in the past. You hope others will change and never see yourself as the problem. You're the people who can't let go. You are the ones who claim you forgive, but your actions are controlled by how they treated you in the past. You might be depressed and can't move forward.

You are the people thinking this is all you deserve. You are the co-dependents looking for approval. You are the ones that stay in one place and afraid to move. You are the ones addicted to drama, so you remain in hopeless situations that will never change. You remain in impossible relationships hoping they will change. You visit depressed because you refuse to get the help you need. You cling to your hope of what will make you happy!

You are the older people who have never grown up. You might be a drug addict or alcoholic, and yes, a little pot once in a while bunch. Reading this paper, you might ask yourself, how does he know about these people? I know because God has delivered me from all this dysfunction.

DO YOU KNOW THE TRUTH?

I understand how depression can make us feel alone. I can relate to you because, at times, I still feel oppressed. I spent a short lifetime crushed, receiving only moments of being happy. Watching my son, I see how dysfunction can destroy a person's life.

I was in bad relationships; I have hurt people because I couldn't let go. I was selfish and only thought about getting the things I want, and yes, the whole time, I thought, if only others would change.

I would read self-help books, went to therapy, and started going to a new age church. I thought my life was going in the right direction. The whole time I was searching for a god of my understanding. How can you find God when you are busy being God?

In reality, many people live this way, but somehow we hold on, hoping to hope that never changes. You hang on to expectations, but while you wait, you are never happy. You never feel the joy Jesus can give you!

You stay in relationships that will hurt you. You pick people you are attracted to and hope this time it will be different. You are the martyrs of the world. You look for love in all the wrong places. Stay in bad relationships thinking this is all you deserve!

I was truly blind and couldn't see I was hurting others and myself. I was digging a hole that kept getting deeper. I spent thirty years of my sober life hoping some loved ones would come back. How can anyone be joyful when we live our lives this way?

Jesus can give you choices. You can stay oppressed, the question God is asking you, "Are you sick and tired of living this way?" Are you tired of being oppressed?

God doesn't belittle the pain you might be going through. He wants to be a part of your life and gives you choices that can lead to eternal freedom. You learn to be happy even if you don't get the things you want!

I say these things so you realize I have been there. I lived that way for my entire life; it was only because of Jesus and His grace and mercy that I can claim victory. Now, God uses my experience to understand and help others to find Jesus.

At Mount Sinai, God made a covenant with Moses, and He wanted to pass that covenant on to the Israelites and, eventually, the Gentiles(everyone). At that time, He gave Moses the Ten Commandments. If the people didn't break His laws, He would be faithful and keep His covenant with the people. When the Israelites refused to obey His commandments, the only way God could bring them back is to teach them a lesson. He would abandon them and leave them oppressed. Can you imagine how much suffering could have been avoided by following God's Ten commandments?

Pain leads to growth; Your willpower only leads to failure! Jesus wants you to grow and gives you the ability to learn your lessons! He doesn't want you to make the same mistakes and expect different results!

We are truly blessed because Jesus gave us a chance to repent and to be forgiven. God doesn't want our generation to feel oppressed. The same God who made a covenant with Moses is the same God who wants to make a covenant with you. Many in the world today face oppression daily because of the decisions they make. Jesus can show you a way of life that can deliver you from being oppressed. Even people placed in situations out of their control can find comfort by following Jesus.

Listening to Joyce Meyer shows me how God carried her through some horrible times in her childhood. Now she uses her experience to help others. I hear testimonies all the time about the power of God and how He changed their lives completely.

I have a suggestion for you that can change your life forever. If you want to quit feeling oppressed:

1. Find a good church, and go up to the altar and pray.
2. Take all your misery and oppression and put it at the foot of the cross, and ask God to fill you with the Holy Spirit.

3. Ask God to be your Lord and Savior. If you continue seeking God and asking Him to help you make decisions, He will listen and guide you.

Jesus can give you a life filled with purpose and meaning. If you are tired of being oppressed, Jesus can give you choices. Your oppression can last a lifetime; asking Jesus to be in your life can lead to eternal freedom!

CHAPTER 26

Feed My Sheep

Abraham, Moses, Mary, Joseph, David, Nehemiah, even Jesus: God had a plan for all these people. Nothing man tried doing could stop God's plan. For many people in the world today, God is calling you to be a part of His purpose.

Psalm 16:7-8: "I will praise the LORD, Who counsels me; even at night, my heart counsels me, I have set the LORD always before me. Because He is my right hand, I will not be shaken." David knew God was his right-hand man. He knew only God could help him to make the right decisions.

There is a stigma that many attach to Jesus; unbelievers think they have to change after they meet Jesus. Jesus didn't come down to take your life away, but to give you eternal life. Even if you are gay, poor, a prisoner in jail, or going through hard times, God wants you to be part of His salvation. The Bible teaches us a practical way that will lead your soul to eternal freedom. Seeing yourself in God's eyes will lead you to make better decisions. The Holy Spirit will shine on your life, and you will see things differently.

I fought with depression for many years; it's no wonder I couldn't understand God and how He could help me. After finding Jesus and His Spirit-filled mine, I could let go of my depression. I made Jesus my right-hand man, and my thought patterns began to change. God gave me a choice on a better way to live my life. I didn't have to change; I wanted to!

Luke 9:23: "Then He said to them all: If anyone comes after Me, he must deny himself and take up his cross daily and follow me." Being powerless and having to start over seemed hopeless. I knew my decisions would cost me more heartache and pain. God gave me a choice and a way of life(Jesus) that would lead to freedom. Verse 24 continues by Jesus' saying, "For whoever wants to save his life will lose it, but whoever loses his life for Me will save it."

Verse 25, Jesus asks us a question: "What good is it for a man to gain the whole world, and yet lose your very self?" Jesus is talking about our soul; the soul determines the journey we choose to follow. Ecclesiastes 12:7: " and the dust returns to the ground it came from, and the Spirit returns to God who gave it." Our earthly bodies turn to dust, but one day our soul will return to God.

Matthew 6:19-21: "Do not store up for yourselves treasures on earth, where moth and vermin destroy, and thieves break in and steal. But store up treasures in heaven, where thieves do not break in and steal. For where your treasure is, there your heart will also be."

What I thought brought me happiness only would bring more pain. God doesn't want us to be weak, but He doesn't want money, possessions, or relationships to be the source of all our happiness. God wanted me to store up treasures that lead my soul toward freedom.

Making decisions that pulled me closer to God would lead to good results. When we do a thing for the right reasons, we get blessings in return. We can't outgive the treasures that God can give us. Jesus is building up everyone He calls, and He(Holy Spirit) is making them worthy to be called a disciple.

John 21:15: "When they had finished eating, Jesus said to Simon Peter, 'Simon, son of John, do you truly love me more than these? 'Yes Lord,' he said, you know I love You. Jesus said, 'Feed My lambs.'"

Jesus asked Peter three times, "do you love Me.". Peter responded three times by saying he loves Him. Jesus' response; Feed My lambs. Take care of My Sheep. Feed My sheep. If we are a disciple, we will feed God's sheep.

1 Peter 4:7-11: "The end of all things is near. Therefore be clear-minded and self-controlled so that you can pray. Above all, love each other deeply because love covers a multitude of sins. Offer hospitality to one another without grumbling. Each other should use whatever gift he has received to serve others, faithfully administrating God's grace in its various forms. If anyone speaks, he should do it as one speaking the very words of God. If anyone serves, he should do it with the strength God provides, so that in all things, God be praised through Jesus Christ our Savior. To Him be the glory and the power forever and ever. Amen."

Our attitude to others shows them we are different. We treat them with love; we use the gifts God has given us to help others. We truly feed the sheep by the way we conduct our affairs. You can call yourself a Christian, but a disciple truly helps others that God places in his path. I think all Christians should ask themselves, "Am I a disciple?" Do I use the gifts God has given me to help others? Do I feed the sheep?

2 Timothy 4:6: " For I am already poured out like a drink offering and the time has come for my departure." Paul knew his time to die would be soon; a drink offering is a wine sprinkled on an altar as a sacrifice(Genesis 35:14.) Jesus stopped Paul on his journey to Damascus; Paul spent a lifetime pouring out God's Spirit to anyone who crossed his path.

Verse 7, "I fought the good fight, I finished the race. I have kept the faith." Paul compared his life following Jesus to a race he was running. Paul knew his life on earth was momentary compared to the eternity he would spend with Jesus.

Verse 8, "Now there is in store for me, the crown of righteousness, which the Lord, the righteous Judge, will award to me on that day--and not only to me, but also to all who have longed for His appearing."

DO YOU KNOW THE TRUTH?

Many of us spent a lifetime running. Accepting Jesus as our Savior would lead to running a different race. The verses above aren't saying we are perfect, that we will never make mistakes. Paul fought the good fight, which means whatever he faced would keep his eyes on Jesus and completing his purpose. In good and bad times, he still finished his race and kept the faith. Even if times are wrong, we can inspire people we know by keeping the faith. Paul used his pain to encourage and help people that are struggling.

God knows if we are trying to be the best person we can be, that doesn't mean we are human, and at times we fall short of righteousness. Despite our imperfections, Jesus doesn't want us to feel unworthy of His love. Regardless of the world(circumstances) around us, He wants us to finish our race!

CHAPTER 27

A Living Sacrifice (ESV)

Romans 12: 1: "I appeal to you therefore, brothers, by the mercies of God, to present your bodies as a living sacrifice, holy and acceptable to God, which is your spiritual worship." After Paul was stopped by God going to Damascus, he became a living sacrifice for Jesus. Jesus was a living sacrifice and paid the ultimate price by dying on the cross. He lowered Himself and became a servant, through His example, showed us a way to live.

Verse 2a: "Do not be conformed to this world, but be transformed by the renewal of your mind." If God calls us, then we will be drawn to Jesus. When we feel the Holy Spirit fill our soul, a transformation begins to happen. The renewal of the mind! 2b, "by testing you may discern what is the will God, what is good and acceptable and perfect." You begin to see God's will, and you begin to discern the world's ways and how they conflict with God's ways.

Being a living sacrifice isn't a life sentence. We are open to learning. We surrender and what Jesus teaches us only makes us stronger. We are not doormats to society. God wants us to enjoy our lives regardless of our circumstances.

God's ways are pleasing and perfect; He wants to transform and develop our minds. By being living sacrifices, we are willing to let Jesus be a service to us, and we learn how our service can draw people to God.

Verse 6, we are one body in God's eyes, but we all are different; we are given gifts, together they work as one in His body. Prophesy, service, giving financially, and leaders God gives everyone He calls gifts, and we use them to form His body, the church.

Verse 9, "Let love be genuine, abhor what is evil; hold fast to what is good." At the center of our being, Jesus wants us to be loving. God wants our love to be genuine, be disgusted with evil, and learn to be faithful to His truth.

Verse 11a, "Do not be slothful in zeal. Don't become lazy and complacent. 11b, "Be fervent in spirit, serve the Lord. Even at times of trouble, keep your eyes on God. Verse 12, "Rejoice in hope, be patient in tribulation." We cling to God and His Word, and God wants us to be patient; when tribulation comes, know He is still in control.

Verse 16, "Live in harmony with one another." Learn how to create harmony with the people around you, even the people we find hard to be around. "Do not be haughty, but associate with the lowly." Don't be haughty, don't be arrogant thinking you are above anyone. "Never be wise in your own sight." Don't talk above others, making them think how wise you are. Talk so they can understand what you are saying.

Verse 17, "Repay no one evil for evil, but give thought to what is honorable in the sight of all." Don't react, set a good example, always try to be kind and peaceful. Verse 20a, "If your enemy is hungry feed him; if he is thirsty give him something to drink. Show them love and be patient 20b; by doing this, you pour burning coals on his head. All these things listed above are the marks of a true Christian, a person willing to be one of God's disciples.

Verse 19, we are reminded not to be vengeful; it is written, "Vengence is mine." When we feel someone has harmed us, don't become vengeful. People spend a lifetime being angrily unable to move forward, and they fail to see the blessings Jesus can put into their lives. Anger puts a sentence on our spiritual selves!

Paul was stoned, put in prison; the world says, "He had every right to become angry." The Holy Spirit helped Paul use his anger in the right way. While in prison, he would write thirty percent of the New Testament. Those letters to the church still encourage us at times of trouble. Millions of people throughout humanity are making Jesus their Lord and Savior; can so many be wrong?

Romans 13:1: "Let every person be subject to the governing authorities. For there is no authority except from God, and those that exist have been instituted by God." Wow! What a pill for many of us to believe. Are we going to spend 2021 blaming the democrats for the decisions they will make? Will this help us or put a sentence on ourselves? We might disagree with their choices, but we still respect who God puts in authority.

Romans 13:2-3: "Therefore whoever resists the authorities resists what God has appointed, and those who resist will incur judgment." How we reacted to authority in the past, how our attitude would pass judgment on ourselves, God wants us to accept those He puts in charge. Even if we don't like them, pray for them; pray that they make the right decisions.

Verse 5, "Therefore one must be in subjection, not only to avoid God's wrath but also for the sake of conscience." If we are not subjective, we can become angry, resentful, and pass judgment on ourselves, and can't move forward. If we want our conscience to be clear, we learn to accept what God has placed in authority.

Verse 12-14: "The night is far gone, the day is at hand. So let us cast off the works of darkness and put on the armor of light." The day of God's coming is near, and God wants us to be clean on the inside. "let us walk properly as in daylight, not in orgies and drunkenness, not in sexual immorality and sensuality, not in quarreling and jealousy."

Jesus wants us to look at our attitudes; hatred leads to murder, jealousy leads to strife and lust to adultery. Verse 14: "Put on the Lord Jesus Christ and make no provisions of the flesh, to gratify its desires."

DO YOU KNOW THE TRUTH?

The day is approaching when we will meet our Savior; when that day comes, He wants us to be pure on the inside. Learning to look inside ourselves and learning to put it in the light is key to growth. I truly hurt others while chasing my desires; Jesus is teaching me to be unselfish, not to cause others pain and suffering. Jesus is teaching me the true meaning of love.

Philippians 3:15: "Let those of us who are mature think this way, and if anything you think otherwise, God will reveal that also to you." Listen to the Holy Spirit and what He is saying. Verse 16: "Only let us hold true to what we have attained." Being a living sacrifice, when the going seems complicated, "Don't quit believing!"

Do you understand the importance of being a living sacrifice? How your behavior hurt you and others?

Are you willing to work toward change?

Has finding Jesus helped you improve in some areas that once were weak?

CHAPTER 28

Keep Your Eyes On Me

Paul had invited his friend to come to our Bible study. Jim was diagnosed with fourth-stage cancer in his lungs. Jim was a big part of helping our church in the transition of change. We never knew a lot of things about Jim; he never bragged about himself or his accomplishments.

We were to meet and introduce ourselves. I thought, what could I say to this man who was fighting cancer. Going to work, I was listening to this song, and God answered my prayer. The verses spoke volumes to me. Whenever my world is falling apart, "Keep your eyes on me." In times of indecision and hurt, "Keep your eyes on me." When members of my family are sick, "Keep your eyes on me." When you have done all you can do, given all that you have to give, said as much as you can say, "Keep your eyes on me." That became the topic of this paper. That was the topic I would bring up for discussion.

Job 2:7-10: "So Satan went out from the presence of the Lord and afflicted Job with painful sores from the soles of his feet to the top of his head. Then Job took a piece of broken pottery and scraped himself with it as he sat among the ashes. His wife said to him, 'Are you still holding on to your integrity?' Curse God and die!" He replied, 'You are talking like a foolish woman.' Shall we accept good from God and not trouble?" Job did not deny God's presence; he would "Keep his eyes on God."

DO YOU KNOW THE TRUTH?

The question I was posing to the people gathered together that night was simple: When we have trouble or sickness in our life, do we use this opportunity to draw us closer to God? Or do we deny the presence of God, who can keep us moving forward? There are always friends, even our loved ones, who give us their opinions, but the bottom line, "Do I keep my eyes on God?" Do I understand by leaning on Him? He will always give us what we need?

John 1:3-5: "Through Him, all things were made; without Him, nothing was made that has been made. In Him was life, and that life was the light of men. The light shines in the darkness, but the darkness has not understood it."

No situation is too challenging for God to handle. I know Jim's faith in God was strong. We could always feel hope when we were around him.

The last Bible study we had with him, I remember one of the last things he said, "I never felt closer to God than the way I feel today." Jim gave us so much more than what we gave him. You beat cancer by not giving up. He passed away two weeks later. Jim never considered himself to be a victim; he showed us how to be a survivor.

Romans 8:28: "And we know in all things God works for the good of those who love Him, who have been called according to His purpose." Situations happen in our life, situations God couldn't control. I lost family members, I know how their deaths could have been avoided, but they happened.

For a long time, I couldn't understand why God allowed them to happen. Two of those deaths would lead to my sobriety. I have been sober for forty years. God uses my experience to help others.

Later on, my step-daughter's death would lead to making Jesus, My Lord and Savior. We never know what good can come out of tragedies that have happened in our lives. Knowing Jim, he taught me how to keep my eyes on God. Sometime on this journey, I will use that experience to help God and His purpose. Jim taught me how to handle adversity.

Jesus can't always control the storms that can come into our lives. If we put our faith in Him, He can give us the confidence to keep moving forward. I remember a book I read years ago. The title, "Why bad things happen to good people." A Jewish rabbi wrote this book after his son died of a rare disease at a young age. The purpose of the book was to let people know, bad things happen to good people. God doesn't do those things, but they still can happen.

I was like the Rabbi; whenever bad things happened, I would blame God and use it to avoid Him. Just like the Rabbi was blaming God for his son's death, I blamed God for all the bad things in my life. Finding Jesus, I had to put my prejudice aside, and I started to see God in a different light.

God gave us a free choice. God can't control the options of people. At any time, we can become a victim of someone's insanity. People make choices on how they want to live their lives.

We can deal with anger by being forgiving, or our passion can turn to resentment and hate. We can blame people for an entire lifetime, be victims, or grow up and take responsibility. We can handle pain on our own, stay up all night, worry, or learn to trust God. We can feel guilty or ask God for His forgiveness. Finding Jesus gave me the freedom to make choices that would lead to eternal freedom. Jesus has given me a strong foundation.

Finding Jesus, I was given a choice on how to let go. I have the wisdom to know what I can't handle and give it to God. I know God can overcome dire situations and keep us moving forward. Instead of blaming God, I keep my eyes on God. I go to Him, knowing He is more significant than what is in the world!

CHAPTER 29

Thank You, Jesus

My life was falling apart. I prayed to God, asking Him to help me. Lord, if you want me to receive your Spirit, then I am ready to receive it. With my arms open and raised, Jesus sent down the Holy Spirit; I felt His presence inside me! I walked out of the Bible study, knowing my world had changed. His Spirit made me feel healthier.

Even when I fail, I can go to Him and ask for forgiveness. If I don't feel worthy of His love, I know He still loves me. When I think I'm not any good, I hear the Spirit inside telling me, "I love you, and I won't give up on you."

I know my faults, but still, He says, "I love you just the way you are." My shortcomings, the failures, this is who I am; He accepts me. Even though we all have sinned and fall short of His glory, He wants us to be a part of God's family.

God sent down, His only begotten Son, and His name is Jesus. He died for the sins we committed, and three days later, He would rise and conquer death. Jesus paid the ultimate price for the sins of humanity and made the path clear, so God, His Father, says, "You are forgiven."

Jesus promised the apostles before His death, the Counselor(Holy Spirit) could come down and fill our souls. God knew if people couldn't receive the Spirit, they would fail and fall short of their redemption. God wants us to take all the hurt and pain that we are feeling, and lay it down at the foot of Jesus' cross, and ask Him for forgiveness.

I know how His Spirit inside you can change your life. The only way is by asking Him to be your Savior. I can only imagine what God has waiting for those who put their trust in Him.

I pray for anyone who has doubts; I implore you to hear God's calling. The virus is causing heartache, but God knows how you suffer and wants to help you. You have lost some loved ones, some of you watched your business fall, some are in homes waiting for all this to an end; I pray you to ask God for help. I pray that any people lacking faith look inside their hearts and ask Jesus to come into their lives.

I pray they have a moment of clarity, and God's light begins to give them hope. I pray from this small beginning; you start to build a strong foundation, knowing someone is there who can help you.

I see how the virus is bringing out the best or the worst in people. Parts of the world are under civil unrest, and at times it all seems to be falling apart. I pray that Christians know that God is still in control. I pray for God's disciples to make calls and try to help people who need their help.

I pray we take this time to learn any lessons that God wants us to know. If there is any prejudice in our hearts that we ask God for forgiveness. Take the time to understand others by putting yourself in their lives. Take the time to see what we value and if your faith is weak, take the time to draw closer to God!

Everyone has a journey, a beginning, a middle, and for some, the end. Start a journey that will last for an eternity. We are on earth for only moments of our life, but eternity goes on even after we die. 1 Chronicles 28:10: "Be careful now, for the Lord has chosen you to build a house for the sanctuary, be strong, and do it." David is challenging Solomon to build a temple for God. God is telling people who seek to follow Him to build a temple inside themselves, a foundation worthy of Jesus' presence!

Verse 20: "Then David said to his son, 'Be strong and courageous and do it.' Do not be afraid and do not be dismayed, for the Lord God, even my God is with you. He will not leave or forsake you until all the work for the service of the house of the Lord is finished." The same promise that David gave Solomon is the same promise God is giving us. Jesus and the Holy Spirit won't leave or forsake us while working on our lives and a new foundation.

2 Chronicles 7:14: "If my people, who are called by My name, will humble themselves and pray and seek My face and turn from their wicked ways, then will I hear from heaven and I will forgive their sin and will heal their land." How often can we hear God's calling and not listen to what He is saying? With all the technology in this country, how can this nation fall so quickly? At times like these, I feel God has pulled His umbrella and has left us. Searching inside my soul for answers, have we abandoned God?

Different cultures and different gods are replacing the Bible, which has been the source of truth. How can people claim to be Christians and read the Bible daily, but your way of thinking opposes all you believe. People are rewriting the word of God so they can feel better about themselves. I pray people to read the Bible, knowing God's truth will help us avoid heartache and pain. I hope people follow the example Jesus has given us.

In 2 Chronicles, God says four things:

1. Be humble.
2. Pray to God for forgiveness.
3. Seek knowledge of His will.
4. Turn away from your sinful behavior.

The Holy Spirit has given me a better understanding of God's truth. When the truth is divided, then bits and pieces are removed. I am thankful Jesus gives all of us a chance to experience eternal freedom. Writing is my way of helping people to gain a better understanding of how God can help you. God can save our nation, and He does that, one soul, at a time.

In conclusion, I feel I have lived two lifetimes, and the end is yet to come. How I lived before I met Jesus and how I asked God forty years ago led to my present journey and making Jesus my Lord and Savior. The end is how my soul spends eternity.

I wrote much of this book at 4:30 in the morning while going through some really dark times in my life. There is a constant theme I often speak about; how God saved me. I wrote this book hoping to reach new people. I wanted people to know how God can help them and the way He answers all our needs.

CHAPTER 30

God's Answer To the World

To the Alcoholic, the answer lies in the bottom of the bottle; the answer lies in drowning out your pain. Alcohol gives you wings to fly, but your happiness ends after getting so high. Then you go into a downward cycle and pass out. Many times while drunk, we say and do things that we regret.

To the drug addict, the answer lies in numbing yourself to the world around you. You drag people down who love you. You will do anything to get your drug of choice. When the money runs out, some turn to prostitution, some rob and steal, you end up in institutions, get better, quit doing drugs, but you do nothing to change your personality and end up doing drugs again.

Drinking and doing drugs is a small part of the problem; dealing with our character is 99% of the problem! Continuing to live your old lifestyle only leads you back to doing alcohol or drugs. Jesus, seeking to do His will, will start a journey that will give you purpose and meaning. Jesus provides us with a foundation and a way to live our lives. Instead of building up and tearing down, His way leads to stability.

I spent thirty-five years in AA(Alcoholic Anonymous), I was on the verge of losing another marriage, but I was tired of running. That was when I found Jesus. AA taught me how to quit drinking, I did all the steps, but I wasn't happy. I spent most of my recovery time regretting the past. I had moments of happiness(relationships), but it took years to learn how to let go when they were gone.

Finding Jesus showed me a way of life that would lead to eternal freedom. Finding Jesus helped me to deal with depression and the quilt that was killing me eternally. I learned how to live one day at a time. To appreciate all the things God has given me. Satan no longer has the power to destroy the progress that I am making.

"For God so loved the world that He gave his one and only Son, that whoever believes in Him shall not perish but have eternal life. For God did not send his Son into the world to condemn the world, but to save the world through Him (John 3:16-17.)"

To the recovering addict who asks Jesus to run their lives, God will fill you with the Holy Spirit(Spirit of Truth), and you will gain knowledge that leads to wisdom. Regardless of what happens, God can start to build a foundation. Following Jesus' example will continue to make you stronger.

To the sex addict, the answer lies in the moments of pleasure. One hundred people aren't enough to satisfy your moments of happiness. As a result, you end up hurting yourself and others. You end up in relationships with people who are sicker than you. Sex addicts are insecure people; moments of sex cover up their weaknesses.

Finding Jesus, you can learn how to love yourself and others; you know the opposite sex isn't an object that we can conquer. You remember the right way to getting the things you want.

"Those who hope in the Lord will renew their strength. They will soar on wings like eagles; they will run and not grow weary, they will walk and not be faint (Isaiah 40:31.)" For those who feel alone and depressed, God gives them a promise. "So do not fear, for I am with you; do not be dismayed, for I am your God. I will strengthen you and help you; I will uphold you with my righteous right hand. (Isaiah 41:10)"

Isaiah 53:4-5: "Surely He took up our infirmities and carried our sorrows, but we considered Him stricken by God, smitten by Him, and afflicted. But He was pierced for our transgressions, He was crushed for our iniquities; the punishment that brought us peace was upon Him, and by His wounds, we are healed." Isaiah(prophet) was talking about Jesus. He would come down and make the ultimate sacrifice by dying on the cross for the sins we committed.

To the people who suffer the guilt, Jesus can give you His forgiveness. You will start believing in someone other than yourself; you begin to realize there is someone bigger in your life than the guilt that keeps you from moving forward. Jesus made atonement to God for the sins you committed. If you are genuinely sorry for your sins, change the behavior, "You are forgiven!"

Isaiah 53:6: "We all, like sheep, have gone astray, each of us has turned to our own way, and the Lord has laid on Him the iniquity of us all." We were all intended to be sheep, and God was the Shepherd. But all who come to Jesus have fallen away and went astray.

Jesus took all our iniquity(sins) and laid them on His shoulder. Jesus came down in human form; He knows the meaning of sin, the temptations we face. Jesus understands the human condition and how it keeps us captive. God knew how people would fail and try doing things on their own. God also knew that their brokenness would bring many back to Him!

When you base your hope on getting the things you want, what happens when you don't get those things? Jesus never said we wouldn't get sick. People we love won't walk away. When we suffer because of the human condition, Jesus can always give us what we need. The biggest reason I am writing "do you know the truth" is to let you know you are not alone. Jesus is more significant than any pain that you are feeling. Jesus can save your soul!

Romans 6:23: "For the wages of sin is death, but the gift of God is eternal life in Christ Jesus our Lord." Death is a reality for people's souls who continue making the wrong decisions. Jesus came down to save our souls. Jesus continues to be an answer for people throughout the world. Can so many be wrong after we hear their testimony of how Jesus changed their lives completely?

Instead of removing prayer from our schools or turning our heads because it doesn't affect us, shouldn't we be asking God to help us? Shouldn't we start rallies asking God to heal our nation? How many deaths can we avoid when people begin to realize our children have problems? How many relationships can heal when we start to realize divorce isn't the answer? How can so many be blind when Jesus has a solution?

Mark 4:9: "Then Jesus said, 'He who has ears to hear, let him hear.'" The non-believers wanted signs from God so they couldn't hear what Jesus was saying. They were looking for evidence against Him. We can only hear God if we truly seek to know Him. Many times God is calling, but do you listen to what He is saying?

Romans 8:6-8: "The mind of the sinful man is death, but the mind controlled by the Spirit is life and peace; the sinful mind is hostile to God, does not submit to God's law, nor can it do so. Those controlled by the sinful nature cannot please God."

God can provide us with a way to live our lives. God can give us hope when all hope is gone. How long can we live with our anger and resentment? What does it take for us to realize that our way of living isn't right?

Medicines can heal your sicknesses: Jesus heals our personal lives that need healing. The real world won't always forgive us and the sins we committed. Jesus gives everyone an answer and a way to live life. Regardless of our past, a new beginning. Finally, we come to the churches.

Revelations 2:7: "He who has an ear, let him hear what the Spirit says to the churches. To him who overcomes, I will give the right to eat from the tree of life, which is in the paradise of God." We can go to church but walk out the door an hour later; How do we treat others?

Are we loving and kind? Can we buy our way into heaven? I don't judge people; that is God's ultimate job. To him who overcomes the world and stays on this journey, God has a home waiting for them in heaven.

For those who live the right way, this is a good message for them to hear. God gives those people a new body for their soul, a spiritual body (1 Corinthians 15).

Revelation: 21:7a has a different meaning: "He who overcomes will inherit all this, and I will be his God and he will be my son." Verse 8: "But the cowardly, the unbelieving, the vile, the murderers, the sexually immoral, those who practice magic arts, the idolaters and all liars-- their place is in the fiery lake of burning sulfur. This is the second death." You may think there isn't punishment for people who do wrong, but God has an answer. I don't want people to believe God isn't fair. He knows we will make mistakes and always honor the progress we have made. But for people who live an offensive life, God will judge them as He sees fit.

Jesus didn't punish the world; we do that by living the way we do and the decisions we continue making. Regardless of how far you have fallen, Jesus is waiting with open arms to save you. Do you know the truth? Jesus' truth can set you free!

ABOUT THE AUTHOR

I spent thirty-five years of my sober life helping others. I worked all the steps in Alcoholics Anonymous religiously, but my happiness only lasted for moments. Joy, I thought, meant getting the things I wanted (relationships, money, success); most of the time, I felt alone and depressed. Thirty years sober, I was on the verge of running, going back to doing things on my own, and possibly losing my sobriety. That was when God called me, and I would learn about Jesus, my Lord, and Savior. I was sixty years old when I discovered Jesus.

My life would be meaningless without my relationship with Jesus. I learned Jesus could give me joy regardless of the circumstances in my life. Truth never changes; knowledge of God's word and living by His example gave me spiritual joy. Being manic-depressive and by-polar finding Jesus, I no longer feel alone.

I have been studying the Bible for over ten years. I had so many conceptions and prejudices toward God. Jesus didn't come down to condemn me; He gave me choices on the way I live and feel. Regardless of my circumstances, my age, or how broken I think, Jesus gives you hope!

Regardless of Religion and what others taught you about God, Jesus wants you to have a personal relationship of your own. Following His example will lead to eternal freedom!

www.ingramcontent.com/pod-product-compliance
Lightning Source LLC
Chambersburg PA
CBHW021424070526
44577CB00001B/48